GEDDES & GROSSET

POCKET ATLAS OF
THE WORLD

GEDDES &
GROSSET

2 CONTENTS

4-5	THE WORLD
6-27	NORTH & CENTRAL AMERICA
28-41	SOUTH AMERICA
42-95	EUROPE
96-133	ASIA
134-151	AFRICA
152-165	AUSTRALIA & OCEANIA
166-171	THE POLAR REGIONS
172	INDEX TO MAPS

oads

═══ Motorway/Highway

──── Other Main Road

– at scales smaller than 1:3 million

──── Principal Road: Motorway/Highway

──── Other Main Road

──── Main Railway

owns & Cities – Population

□ > 5,000,000

□ 1-5,000,000

○ 500,000 -1,000,000

○ < 500,000

□ **Paris** National Capital

✈ Airport

──── International Boundary

─ ─ ─ International Boundary – not defined or in dispute

──── Internal Boundary

──── River

⊥⊥⊥⊥⊥ Canal

═══ Marsh or Swamp

Relief

Note –

The 0-100 contour layer appears only at scales larger than 1:3 million

▲ 1510 Peak (in metres)

5000 metres
4000
3000
2000
1000
500
200
100
0
Land below sea level

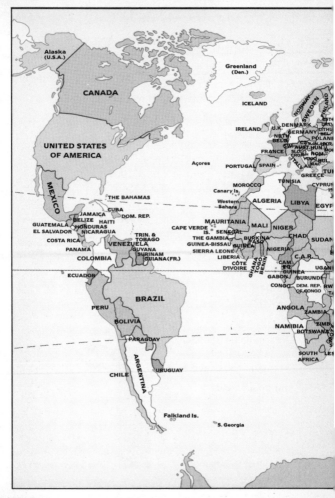

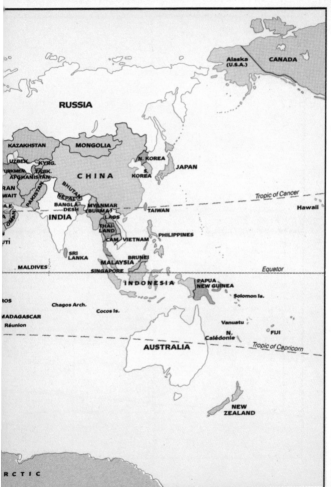

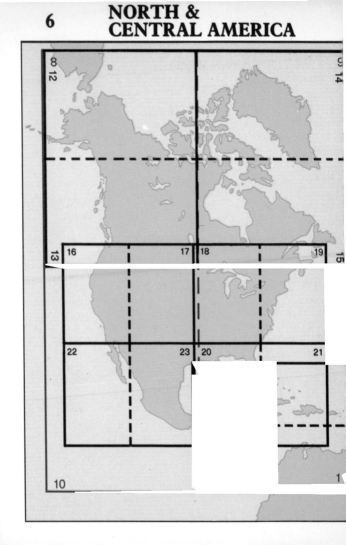

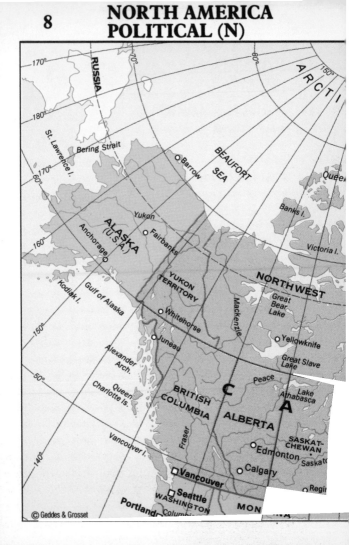

© Geddes & Grosset

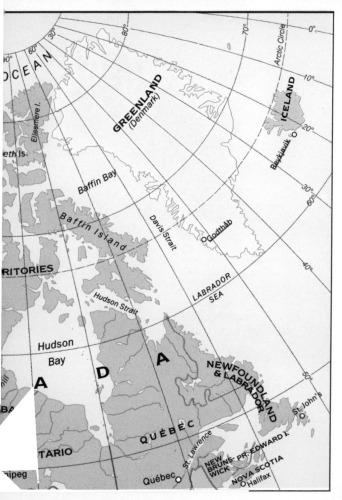

OCEAN

GREENLAND
(Denmark)

ICELAND

Reykjavik O

Arctic Circle

Ellesmere I.

beth Is:

Baffin Bay

Baffin Island

Davis Strait

Qagdthåb

RITORIES

LABRADOR
SEA

Hudson Strait

Hudson
Bay

A

C A N A D A

NEWFOUNDLAND
& LABRADOR

St. John's

ill

A

D

A

BA

QUÉBEC

St. Lawrence

NEW
BRUNS-
WICK

PR. EDWARD I.

NOVA SCOTIA

TARIO

Québec O

O Halifax

nipeg

40°

OREGON   IDAHO   O Helena   Missouri   N. DAKOT

O Boise   O Bism

Snake   WYOMING   SOUTH DAKOTA

Pierre O

Sacramento   Salt Lake City □   Cheyenne O   NEBRASK.

San Francisco □   NEVADA

San José O   CALIFORNIA   UTAH   Linco

Las Vegas   □ Denver   Top

Los Angeles □   UNITED   COLORADO   KANS

San Diego □   ARIZONA   STATES

Colorado   Phoenix □   Albuquerque O

Tucson O   NEW MEXICO   OKLA

El Paso O   Dallas

Rio Bravo del Norte   TEXAS

Austin O

Houst

Rio Grande

Monterrey □

MEXICO

□ Guadalajara

México □

120°   30°   20°   10°

CONN.	CONNECTICUT
DEL.	DELAWARE
M.	MARYLAND
MASS.	MASSACHUSETTS
N.H.	NEW HAMPSHIRE
N.J.	NEW JERSEY
N.Y.	NEW YORK
PENN.	PENNSYLVANIA
R.I.	RHODE ISLAND
VER.	VERMONT

P A C I F I C   O C E A N

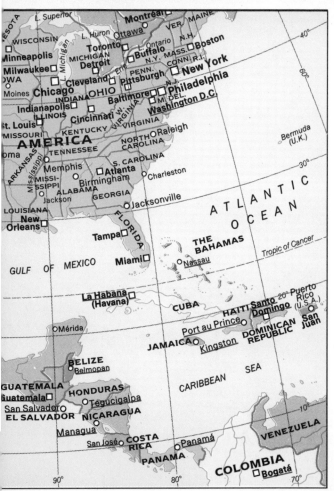

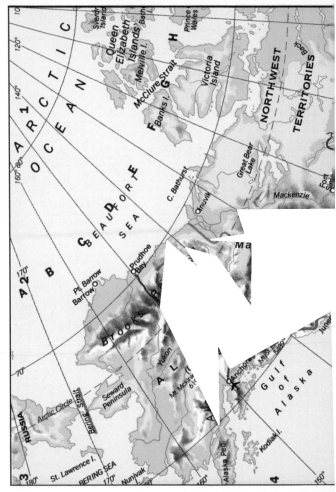

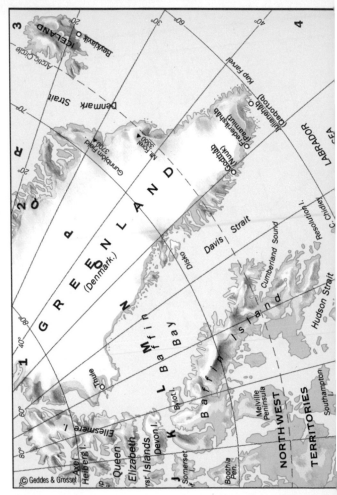

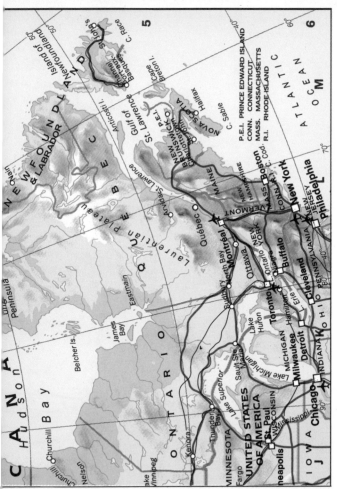

C A N A D A

NEWFOUNDLAND & LABRADOR

Island of Newfoundland

Shoals
C. Race
Portaux Basques
Channelport

Cape Breton I.

Gulf of St. Lawrence

Anticosti I.

C. Sable

N. Vain

Ungava Peninsula

Laurentian Plateau

QUEBEC

NEW BRUNSWICK

NOVA SCOTIA

P.E.I.
Charlottetown

Halifax

St. Lawrence

MAINE

NEW HAMPSHIRE

VERMONT

Québec

Arnprior

Montréal

Ottawa

Sudbury

North Bay

ONTARIO

Toronto

Hamilton

Niagara

Buffalo

NEW YORK

Lake Ontario

L. Erie

Cleveland

PENNSYLVANIA

OHIO

PRINCE EDWARD ISLAND
CONNECTICUT
MASS.   MASSACHUSETTS
CONN.   CONNECTICUT
R.I.   RHODE ISLAND

P.E.I. PRINCE EDWARD ISLAND
CONN.
MASS.
C. Cod.
R.I.
C. Cod.

Boston

MASS.
CONN.

New York

NEW JERSEY

Philadelphia

ATLANTIC OCEAN

M

Hudson Bay

Churchill

Belcher Is.

James Bay

Eastmain

Nelson

Lake Winnipeg

Kenora

Thunder Bay

Lake Superior

Sault Ste. Marie

Lake Huron

Lake Michigan

MICHIGAN

Detroit

Milwaukee

WISCONSIN

MINNESOTA

Fargo

St. Paul

neapolis

IOWA

Mississippi

Chicago

INDIANA

UNITED STATES OF AMERICA

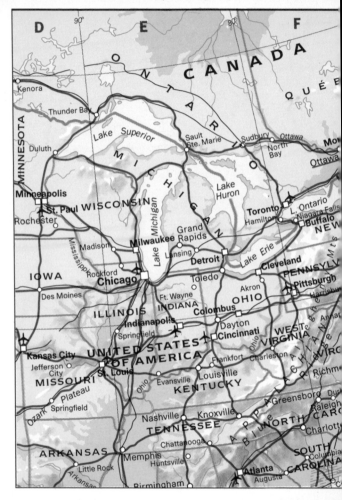

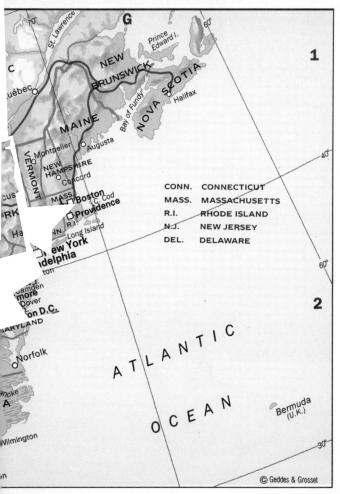

CONN.	CONNECTICUT
MASS.	MASSACHUSETTS
R.I.	RHODE ISLAND
N.J.	NEW JERSEY
DEL.	DELAWARE

ATLANTIC

OCEAN

Bermuda
(U.K.)

© Geddes & Grosset

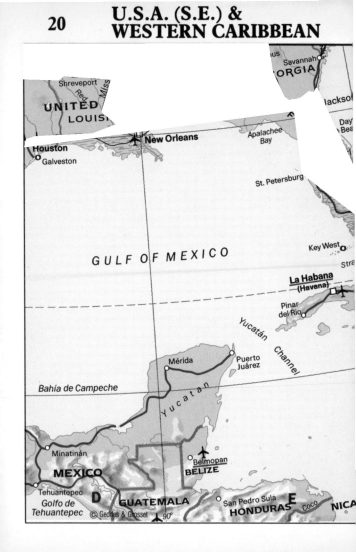

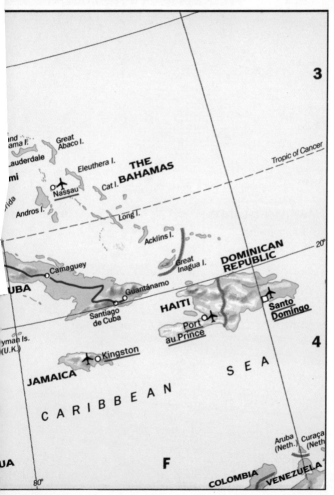

3

... land
...ama I.   Great
Abaco I.

...auderdale   Eleuthera I.   THE
Nassau   Cat I. BAHAMAS

Tropic of Cancer

...mi

...rida   Andros I.   Long I.

Acklins I.

20°

Camaguey   Great
Inagua I.   DOMINICAN
REPUBLIC

CUBA   Guantánamo   HAITI

Santiago
de Cuba   Port   Santo
au Prince   Domingo

...yman Is.
(U.K.)   Kingston   4

JAMAICA   S E A

C A R I B B E A N

Aruba   Curaça
(Neth.)   (Neth

...UA   F

80°   COLOMBIA   VENEZUELA

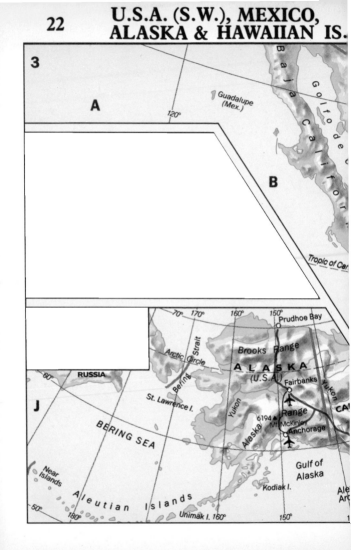

3

A

120°

Guadalupe
(Mex.)

Baja

Golfo de

California

B

Tropic of Car

70°   170°   160°   150°   Prudhoe Bay

Arctic   Strait   Brooks   Range

Arctic Circle   A L A S K A

60°   Bering   (U.S.A.)   Fairbanks   Yukon

RUSSIA

J   St. Lawrence I.   Yukon   Range   CA

6194 ▲   Alaska   Mt. McKinley   Anchorage

BERING SEA

Near
Islands   Gulf of
Alaska

50°   Aleutian   Islands   Kodiak I.   Ale
Arc

180°   Unimak I. 160°   150°

UNITED STATES OF AMERICA

ucson

El Paso

Ciudad
Juárez

Dallas

Fort
Worth

Odessa

Colorado

TEXAS

Brazos

Austin

osillo

Chihuahua

M

Sierra Madre Occidental

Rio Bravo del Norte

Sierra

San Antonio

Los Mochis

E

Laredo

Corpus
Christi

Culiacán

Torreón

Monterrey

Brownsville

Saltillo

Matamoros

Mazatlán

Madre

Aguascalientes

San Luis
Potosí

Tampico

Oriental

Guadalajara

León

Veracruz

México

▲5699
Citlaltépetl

4

C

Puebla

Sierra

Madre

del

Sur

O

Acapulco

C

100°

© Geddes & Grosset

D

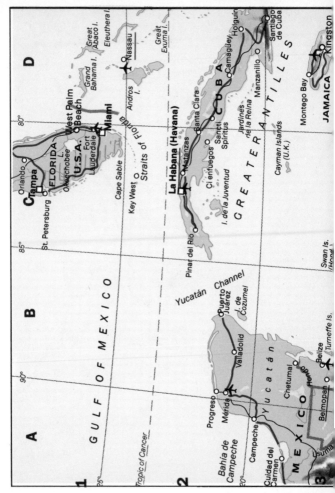

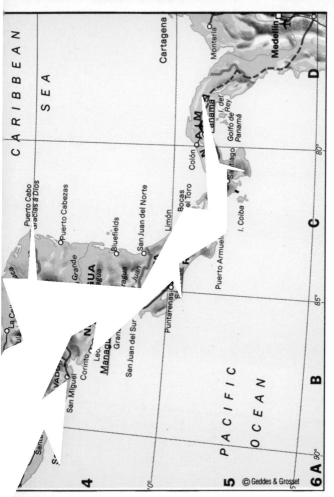

CARIBBEAN

SEA

Cartagena

Montería

Medellín

D

Panamá

I. del

Golfo de Rey

Panamá

80°

Puerto Cabo

racias a Dios

Puerto Cabezas

Colón

antiago

Bluefields

San Juan del Norte

Limón

Bocas

el Toro

C

Grande

EUA

agua

I. Coiba

Puerto Armuell

85°

La C

gua

Juan

Puntarenas

NI

Managua

Leo

Grand

Corinto

San Juan del Sur

PACIFIC

B

San Miguel

VAD

OCEAN

90°

4

5

6 A

© Geddes & Grosset

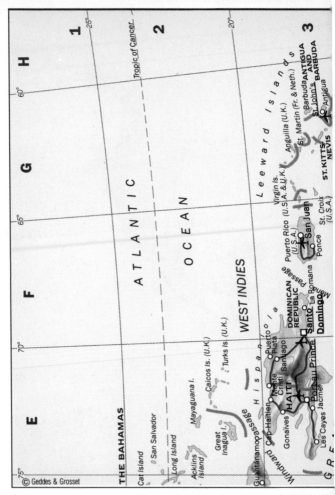

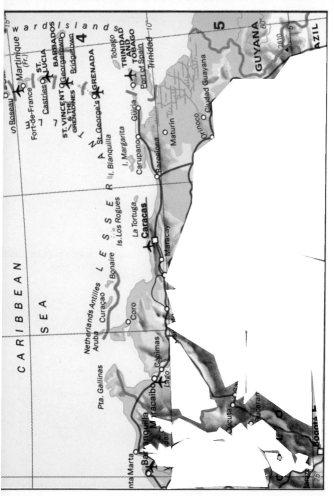

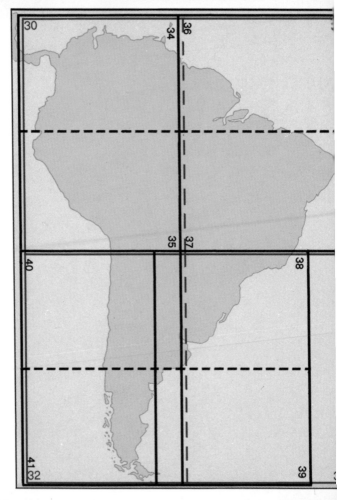

© Geddes & Grosset

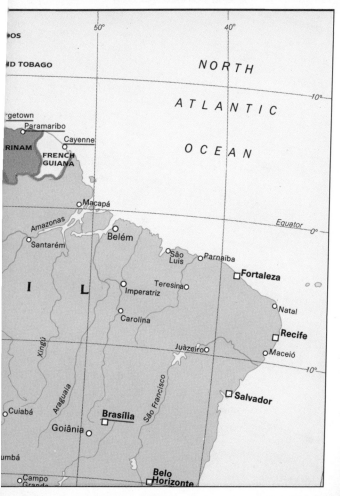

20°

Tropic of Capricorn

Antofagasta

PARA

Salta

San Miguel
de Tucumán

30°

PACIFIC

San Juan

Córdoba

Santa
Fé

Viña del Mar

Santiago

Mendoza

Rosario

Para

OCEAN

C H I L E

ARGENTIN

Concepción

Bahía Bl

NEUQUÉN

Neuquén

90°

40°

Puerto Montt

Comodoro
Rivadavia

Falk
(s. Ma
(U.

50°

Río Gallegos

Est. de
Magallanes
Tierra del
Fuego

Punta Arenas

© Geddes & Grosset

90°

80°

70°

60

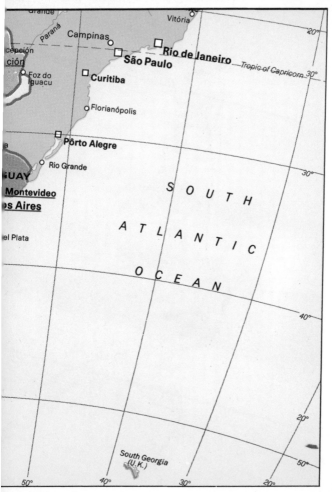

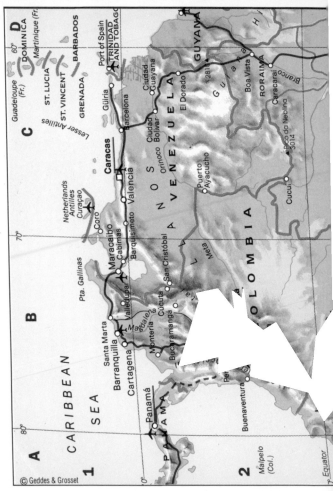

© Geddes & Grosset

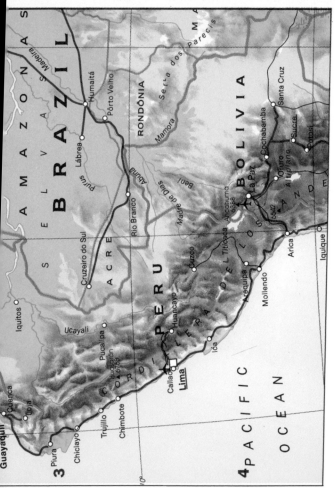

NORTH ATLANTIC OCEAN

Equator

Cayenne

FRENCH GUIANA

Paramaribo

SURINAME

Georgetown

AMAPA

Macapá

lands

© Geddes & Grosset

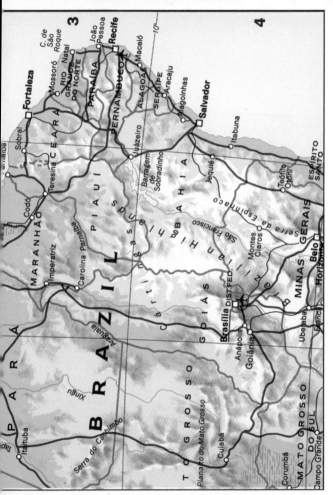

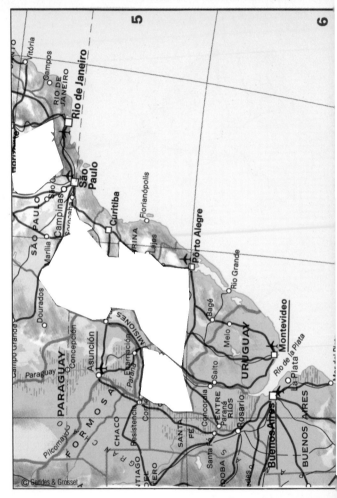

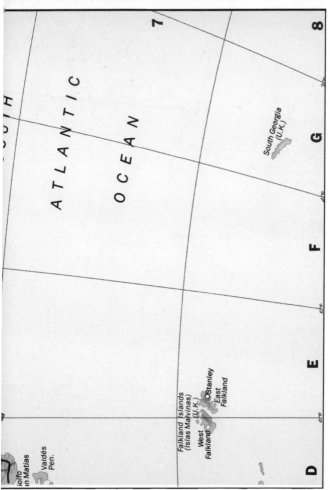

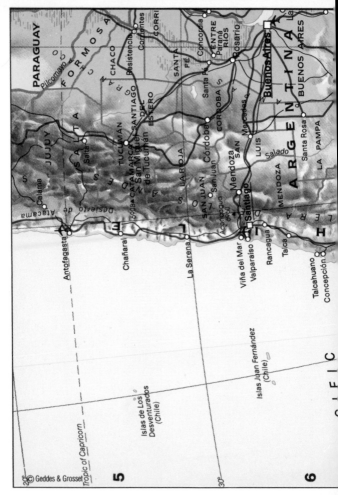

PARAGUAY

CORRIENTES

ARGENTINA

BUENOS AIRES

Buenos Aires

Pilcomayo

FORMOSA

CHACO

Corrientes

Concordia

ENTRE RÍOS

Paraná

Rosario

SANTA FE

Resistencia

JUJUY

SALTA

Salta

Calama

Desierto de Atacama

TUCUMÁN

San Miguel de Tucumán

CATAMARCA

SANTIAGO DEL ESTERO

Santiago

Santa Fe

CÓRDOBA

Córdoba

LA RIOJA

SAN JUAN

San Juan

Mercedes

SAN LUIS

Salado

Santa Rosa

LA PAMPA

Antofagasta

Chañaral

Aconcagua 6960

MENDOZA

Mendoza

Viña del Mar

Valparaíso

Rancagua

Talca

La Serena

Santiago

CHILE

Talcahuano

Concepción

Islas de Los Desventurados (Chile)

Islas Juan Fernández (Chile)

Tropic of Capricorn

PACIFIC

30°

5

6

© Geddes & Grosset

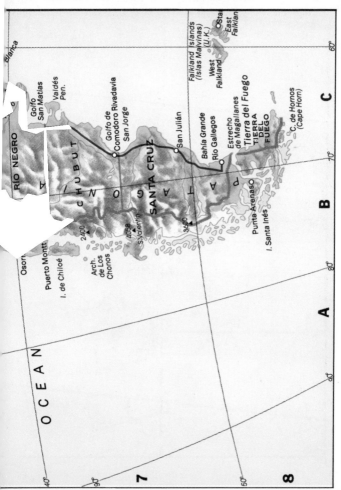

OCEAN

RIO NEGRO

CHUBUT

SANTA CRUZ

PATAGONIA

Blanca

Golfo San Matías

Valdés Pen.

Golfo de San Jorge

Comodoro Rivadavia

San Julián

Bahía Grande

Río Gallegos

Estrecho de Magallanes

TIERRA DEL FUEGO

Tierra del Fuego

C. de Hornos (Cape Horn)

Punta Arenas

I. Santa Inés

Osorno

Puerto Montt

I. de Chiloé

Arch. de Los Chonos

S. Valentín

2400

4058

3600

Falkland Islands (Islas Malvinas)

West Falkland (U.K.)

East Falklan

Sta

60°

70°

80°

90°

40°

50°

C

B

A

7

8

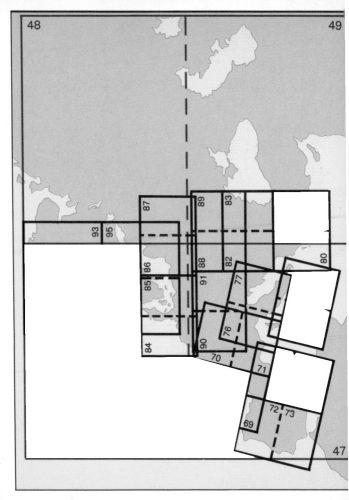

68-69	FRANCE (W)
70-71	FRANCE (E)
72-73	PORTUGAL & SPAIN (W)
74-75	SPAIN (E)
76-77	ITALY (N)
78-79	ITALY (S)
80-81	GREECE
82-83	S.E. EUROPE
84-85	CENTRAL EUROPE (N.W.)
86-87	CENTRAL EUROPE (N.E.)
88-89	CENTRAL EUROPE (S.E.)
90-91	CENTRAL EUROPE (S.W.)
92-93	SCANDINAVIA & THE BALTIC (N)
94-95	SCANDINAVIA & THE BALTIC (S)

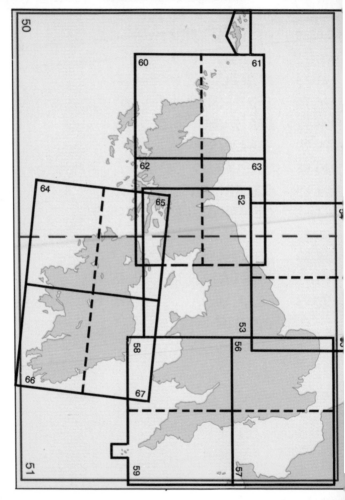

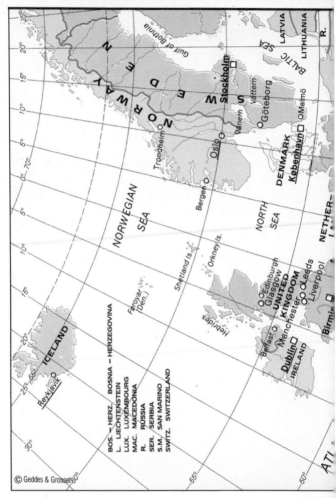

BOS. – HERZ. BOSNIA – HERZEGOVINA
L. LIECHTENSTEIN
LUX. LUXEMBOURG
MAC. MACEDONIA
R. RUSSIA
SER. SERBIA
S.M. SAN MARINO
SWITZ. SWITZERLAND

© Geddes & Grosset

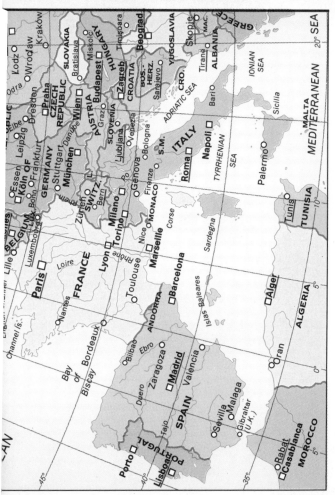

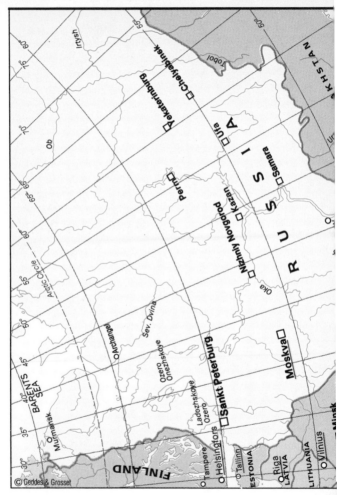

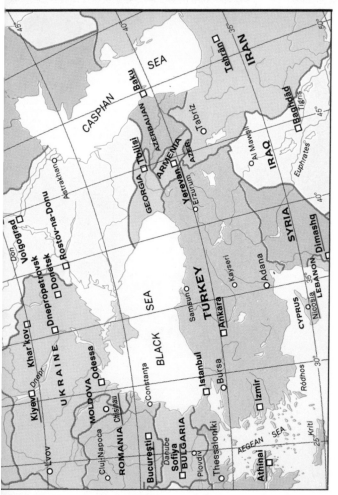

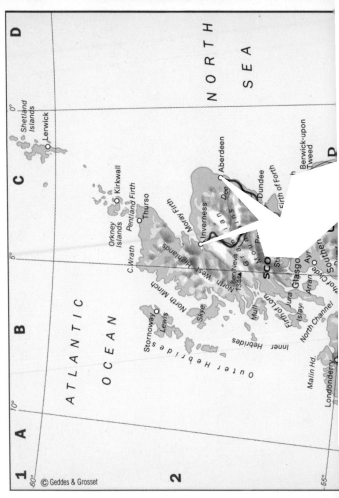

ATLANTIC OCEAN

NORTH SEA

Shetland Islands
Lerwick

Orkney Islands
Kirkwall
Pentland Firth
Thurso
C. Wrath
Moray Firth
Inverness
Dee
Aberdeen
Dundee
Firth of Forth
Berwick-upon-Tweed

Grampian Mountains

Ben Nevis 1344

West Highlands
North Minch
Skye
Outer Hebrides
Lewis
Stornoway
Inner Hebrides
Mull
Firth of Lorn
Jura
Islay
North Channel
Malin Hd.
Londonderry

SCO
Stirling
Glasgow
Ayr
Firth of Clyde
Arran
Southern

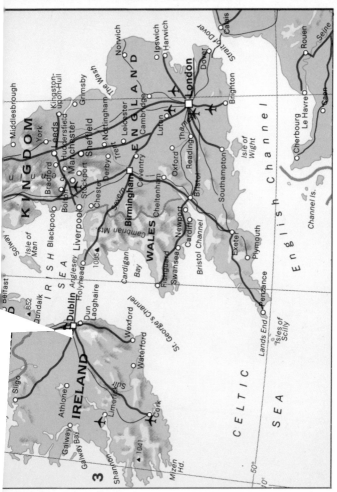

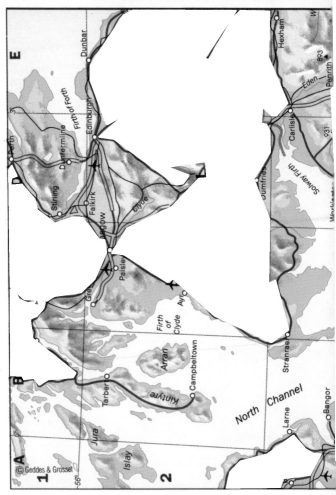

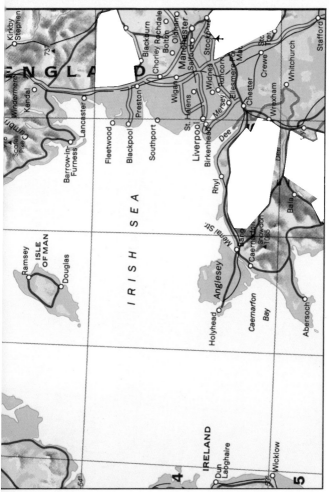

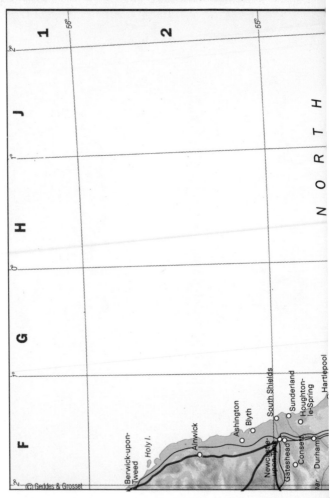

2

54°

4

53°

5

Cromer

S   E   A

Skegness

The
Wash

Flamborough
Head

Bridlington

Kingston-upon-Hull

Spurn Head

Humber

Louth

Boston

Spalding

Scarborough

Scunthorpe

Goole

Ouse

North
York
Moors

Cleveland

E N G L A N D

Ripon

Harrogate

Ure

Wharfe

Keighley

Halifax

Batley

Bradford

Leeds

Castleford

Trent

Leeds

Don

P   e   n   n   i   n   e   s

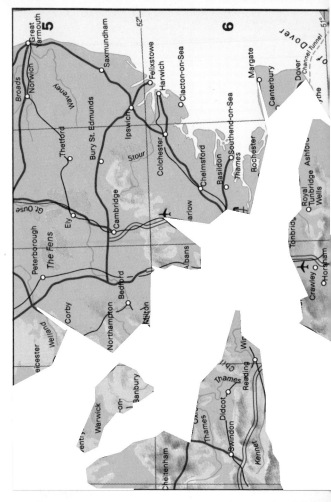

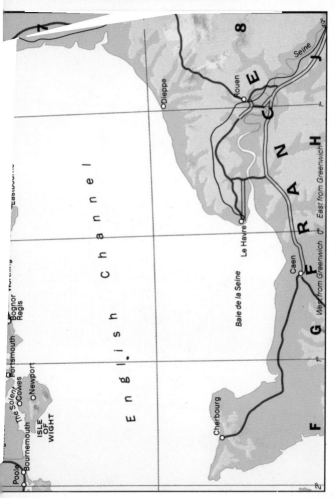

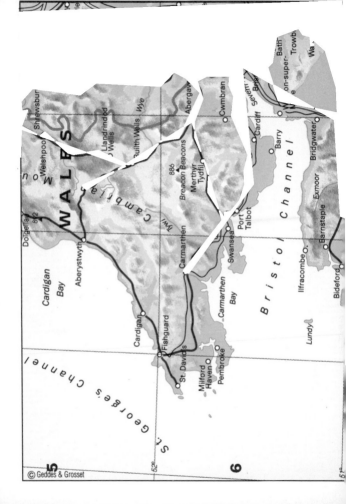

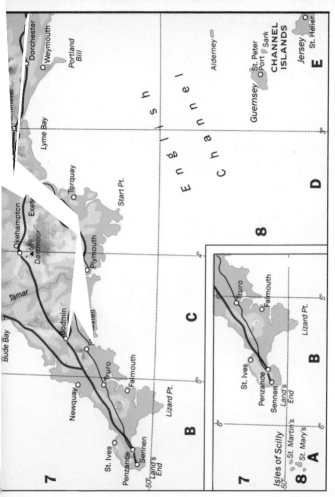

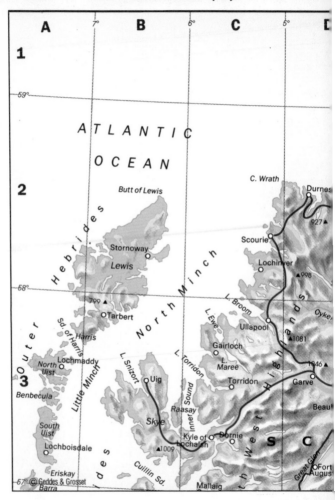

A   7°   B   6°   C   5°   D

ATLANTIC

OCEAN

C. Wrath

Durness

927 ▲

Butt of Lewis

Scourie

Lochinver

Stornoway

▲998

Lewis

Hebrides

North Minch

L. Broom

799 ▲

Tarbert

Oyke

Ullapool

▲1081

Sd. of Harris

L. Ewe

Harris

Gairloch

1946 ▲

L. Torridon

L. Maree

Lochmaddy

Outer

North Uist

N o r t h

Uig

Torridon

Garve

Benbecula

L. Snizort

Beau

Raasay

Little Minch

des

Skye

Kyle of Lochalsh

Dornie

S C

South Uist

▲1009

Lochboisdale

Cuillin Sd.

Mallaig

Great Glen

Fort Augus

Eriskay

Barra

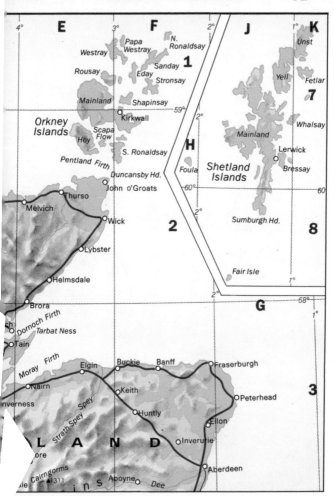

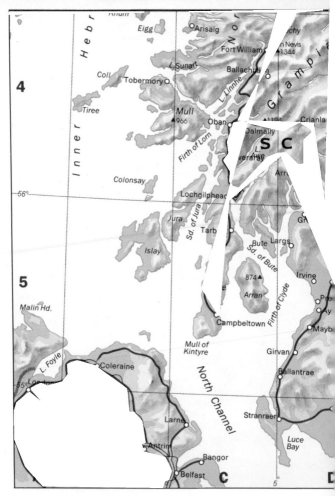

Rhum
Eigg
Arisaig
Fort William
Nevis
1344

4

Coll
Tobermory
Ballachulish
L. Sunart
L. Linnhe

Tiree
Mull
966
Oban
Dalmally
Crianla

Firth of Lorn
S C
L. eraie

Colonsay
Arr

56°
Lochgilphead

Jura
Tarb
Bute
Largs
Sd. of Jura
Sd. of Bute

Islay
874
Irvine

5

Malin Hd.
Arran
Pre
Ay

Campbeltown
Firth of Clyde
Mayb

Mull of
Kintyre
Girvan

L. Foyle
Coleraine
Ballantrae

55°
Lon on

North Channel
Stranraer

Larne
Luce
Bay

Antrim
Bangor

Belfast
C

5

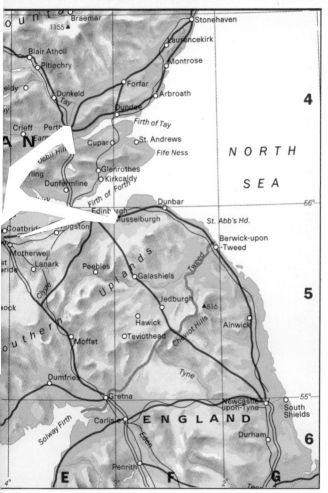

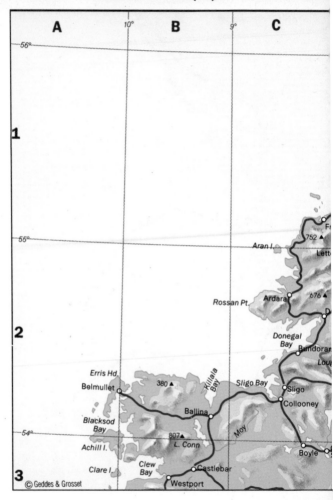

A   10°   B   9°   C

56°

55°

Aran I.

752 ▲   Fr

Lette

Rossan Pt.   Ardara   676 ▲

D

Donegal Bay

Bundoran

Lou

Erris Hd.   380 ▲   Sligo Bay

Belmullet   Killala Bay   Sligo

Ballina   Colloney

Blacksod Bay   Moy

54°

Achill I.   807 ▲   L. Conn   Boyle

Clare I.   Clew Bay   Castlebar

© Geddes & Grosset   Westport

1

2

3

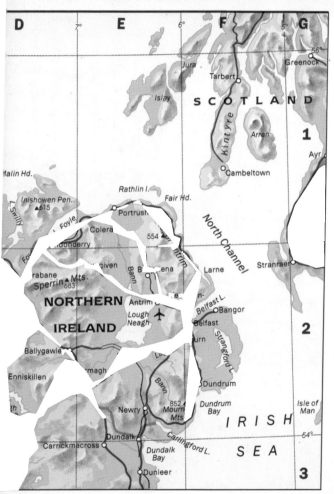

D   E   7°   6°   F   5°   G

56°

Greenock

Jura

Tarbert

Islay

S C O T L A N D

Kintyre

Arran

1

Ayr

Malin Hd.

Inishowen Pen.
▲615

L. Swilly

Rathlin I.

Fair Hd.

Portrush

Colera

L. Foyle

554 ▲

North Channel

Londonderry

Antrim

given

Bann

ena

Larne

Stranraer

rabane

Sperrin ▲ Mts.
683

NORTHERN

Antrim

Belfast L.

IRELAND

Lough
Neagh

OBangor

Belfast

Ballygawle

urn

Strangford L.

2

Enniskillen

magh

Dundrum

Dundee

Bann

Newry

852
Mourn
Mts

Dundrum
Bay

Isle of
Man

I R I S H

Carrickmacross

Dundalk

Carlingford L.

54°

Dundalk
Bay

S E A

Dunleer

3

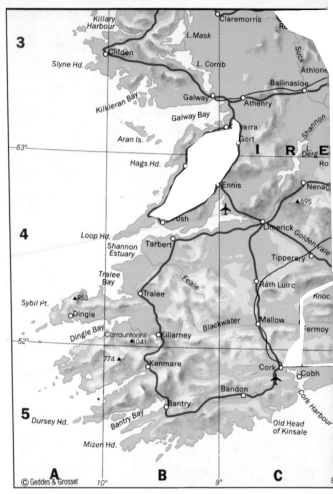

Killary Harbour
Claremorris
L. Mask
3
Clifden
Slyne Hd.
L. Corrib
Suck
Athlone
Ballinasloe
Kilkieran Bay
Galway
Athenry
Galway Bay
Kinvarra
Gort
Aran Is.
I R E
Derg
53°
Hags Hd.
Ro
Ennis
Nenag
▲695
4
Loop Hd.
▲ush
Limerick Golden Vale
Shannon Estuary
Tarbert
Tipperary
Tralee Bay
Feale
Ráth Luirc
Knoc
Sybil Pt.
▲953
Tralee
Dingle
Blackwater
Mallow
Fermoy
52°
Dingle Bay
Carrauntoohil
Killarney
▲1041
774 ▲
Cork
Cobh
Kenmare
Bandon
5
Dursey Hd.
Bantry
Cork Harbour
Bantry Bay
Old Head of Kinsale
Mizen Hd.
© Geddes & Grosset
A
10°
B
9°
C

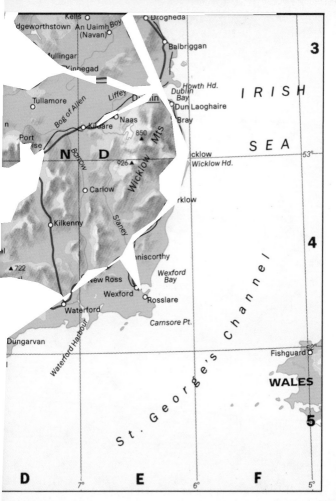

Kells O
dgeworthstown An Uaimh Boy O Drogheda
(Navan) O

Mullingar O Balbriggan

3

Kinnegad

Howth Hd.

I R I S H

Tullamore O Liffey Dublin
Bog of Allen Dublin
Bay

Dun Laoghaire

Naas Bray

n Kildare

Port
ise **N D** 850 ▲ **S E A**

Wicklow 53°
926 ▲ Wicklow Hd.

Kilkenny O Carlow Slaney icklow

4

O Kilkenny

▲ 722 niscorthy

Wexford
New Ross Bay

Wexford O
Waterford O Rosslare

Carnsore Pt.

Dungarvan O Waterford Harbour

Fishguard O 52°

St. George's Channel **WALES**

5

D 7° **E** 6° **F** 5°

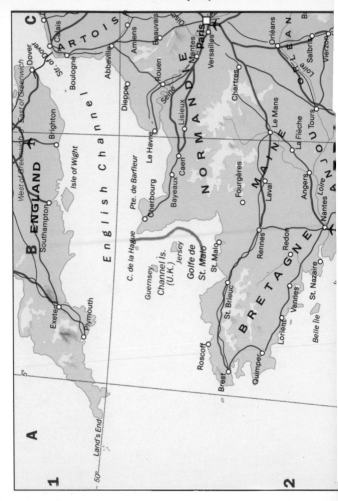

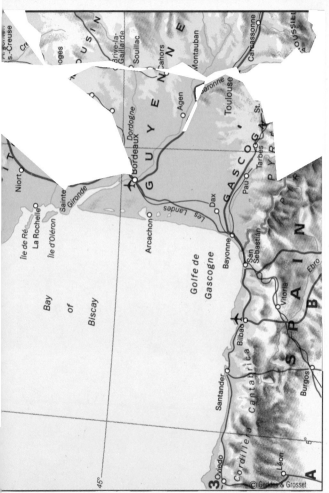

Limousin
s.-Creuse
Crt
oges
Brive-la-Gaillarde
Souillac
Cahors
Montauban
Carcassonne
oussill
GUYENNE
Agen
Garonne
Toulouse
Dordogne
Dordogne
Bordeaux
GUYENNE
GASCO
St.
PYR
Tarbes
Pau
Dax
GASCOGNE
Niort
Sainte
Gironde
Les Landes
Arcachon
Bayonne
San Sebastián
Ebro
Île de Ré
La Rochelle
Île d'Oléron
Golfe de
Gascogne
Vitoria
Bay
of
Biscay
Bilbao
SPAIN
Ebro
Santander
Cantabrica
Burgos
45°
Oviedo
Cordillera
León
A
3

© Geddes & Grosset

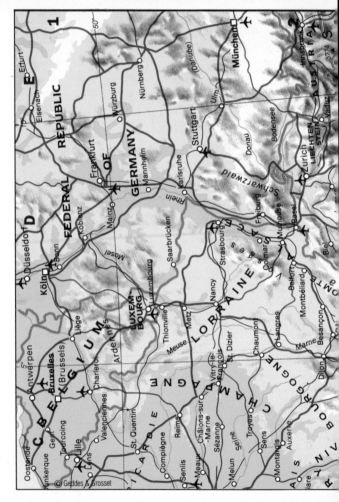

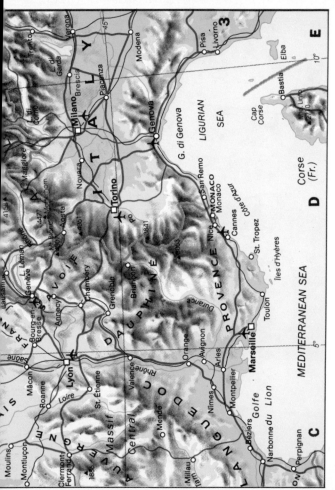

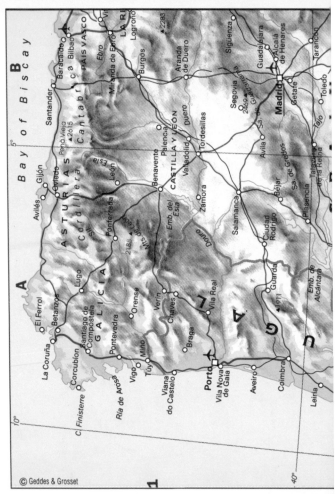

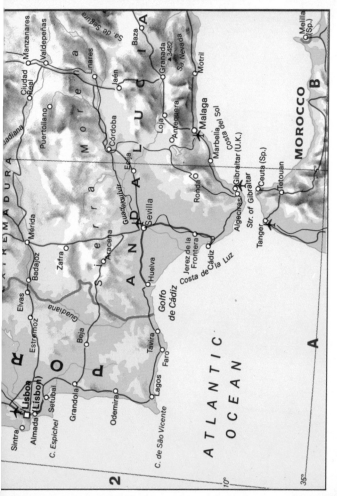

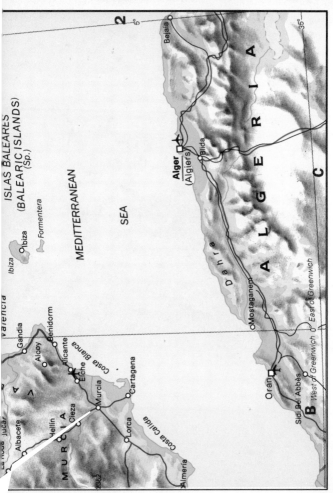

ISLAS BALEARES
(BALEARIC ISLANDS)
(Sp.)

Formentera

Ibiza

Oibiza

MEDITERRANEAN

SEA

ALGERIA

Bejaia

Alger
(Algiers)

Blida

Dahra

OMostaganem

East of Greenwich

Oran

Sidi Bel Abbès

West of Greenwich

B

Valencia

Gandia

Benidorm

Alcoy

Alicante

Elche

Costa Blanca

Murcia

Orihuela

MURCIA

Albacete

Hellin

La Roda

Júcar

Lorca

Cartagena

Costa Cálida

Almería

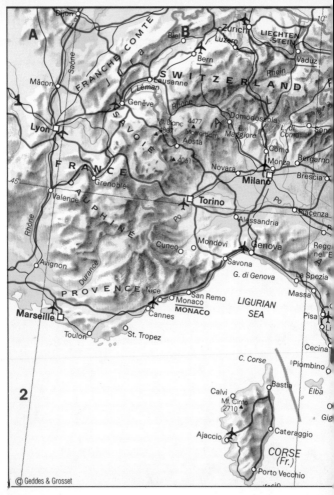

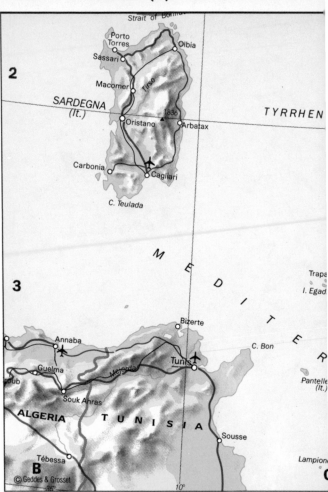

Strait of Bonifacio

Porto
Torres
Olbia
Sassari

2

Macomer
Tirso

SARDEGNA
(It.)
Oristano
1836
Arbatax

TYRRHEN

Carbonia
Cagliari

C. Teulada

M E

D I T

3

E R

Trapa
I. Egad

Bizerte

C. Bon

Annaba
Tunis

R

Guelma
Medjerda

oub
Pantelle
(It.)

Souk Ahras

ALGERIA
T U N I S I A

Sousse

Tébessa
Lampione

© Geddes & Grosset

35°

10°

B

C

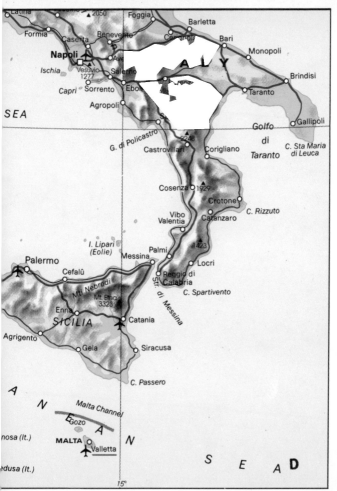

Latina ▲ 2050
Foggia
Barletta
Formia
Caserta Benevente Cerignola Bari
Monopoli
Napoli Ave...
Ischia Vesuvio Salerno I T A L Y Brindisi
1277
Capri Sorrento Ebo... Taranto
Agropoli Gallipoli

SEA Golfo
di C. Sta Maria
G. di Policastro Taranto di Leuca
2248
Castrovillari Corigliano C. Rizzuto
Cosenza 1929
Crotone
Vibo
Valentia Catanzaro C. Rizzuto
1423
I. Lipari Palmi
(Eolie) Locri
Palermo Messina
Cefalù Reggio di
Mti Nebrodi Calabria C. Spartivento
Mt. Etna Str. di Messina
Enna 3328
SICILIA Catania
Agrigento
Gela Siracusa

C. Passero

A
N Malta Channel
E Gozo A
...nosa (It.) N
MALTA Valletta
...edusa (It.) S E A D

15°

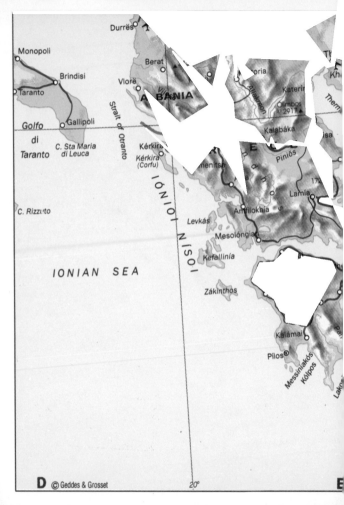

Sea of Marmara
Marmara

Bandirma

Kavála
Alexandroúpolis
Thásos
Samothráki
Gelibolú
K. Strimonikós
Eceabat
B
Gökçeada
ki
K. Sinártikós ▲ 2033
Toronaios
Límnos
Edremi
Áyios
Evstrátios
Ayvalik
T U
Skiathos Iliodhrómia
Lésvos
Skópelos
Skiros
Évvoia
átais
AEGEAN
Khalkis
Khíos
SEA
Izmir
Athínai
(Athens)
Ándros
Sámos
aiévs
Kéa
Ikaría
Tinos
Mikonos
Kíthnos
Síros
Léros
Idhra
KIKLADHES
Kálimnos
Sérifos
Páros
Naxos
Kós
Mirtoan
Sifnos
Amorgós
Sea
Síkinos
Íos
Astípálaia
Mílos
Thíra
Anáfi
eápolis
thira
Sea of Crete
Kárpathos
Khaniá
Kríti
(Crete)
Iráklion
▲ 2456
Akr.
Sídheros
Kásos
Timbákion
F

Dhodhekanisos
Den
3
Muğla
Bodrum
Marmaris
Ródhos
Ródhos
(Rhodes)
Tilos

35°
25°
35°

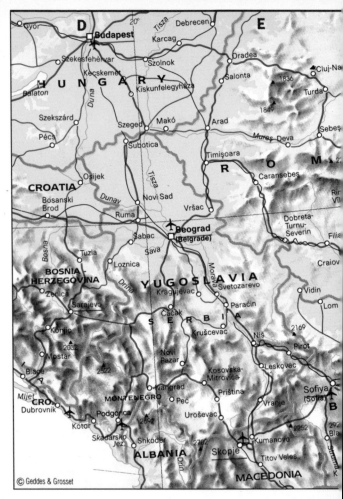

© Geddes & Grosset

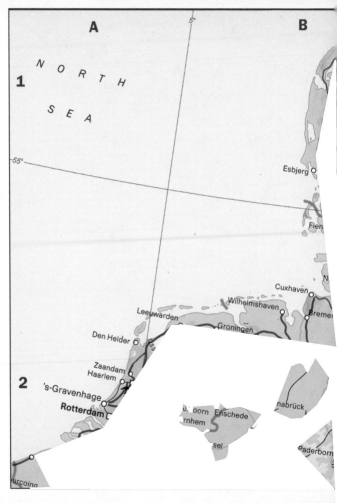

5°

A

B

N O R T H

1

S E A

55°

Esbjerg

Fler

Cuxhaven

Wilhelmshaven

N

Bremen

Leeuwarden

Groningen

Den Helder

Zaandam
Haarlem

2   's-Gravenhage

Rotterdam

oorn   Enschede

rnhem

nabrück

sel

Paderborn

urcoing

D

Visby
Gotland

20°

E Gulf of Riga

25°

Ventspils

Riga

LA

Jelgava

Dvina

Liepãja

BALTIC

SEA

Siauliai

Panevežys

Klaipeda

THUANIA

Ukme

Kaunas

Vilni

Gulf of
Danzig

Kaliningrad

Gusev

Gdynia

RUSSIA

Gdańsk

Elblag

Augustow

Grodno

Olsztyn

Nema

cholskie

Bydgo

Białystok

AND

W.

Bug

Brest

Kobrir

Konin

Warszawa
(Warsaw)

Siedlce

Kalisz

Łódź

© Geddes & Grosset

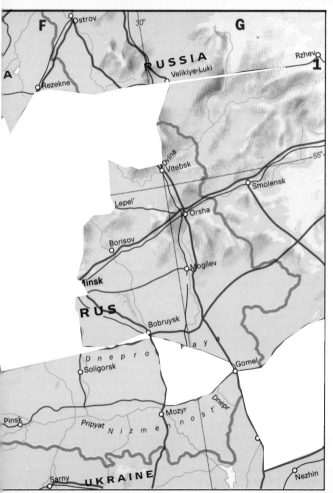

F
Ostrov
30°
G
A
Rezekne
RUSSIA
Velikiye-Luki
Rzhev
1
Dvina
Vitebsk
55°
Smolensk
Lepel'
Orsha
Borisov
Mogilev
Minsk
RUS
Bobruysk
a y a
Gomel
Dnepro
Soligorsk
Dnepr
Pinsk
Mozyr
Pripyat
Nizmennost'
Sarny
UKRAINE
Nezhin

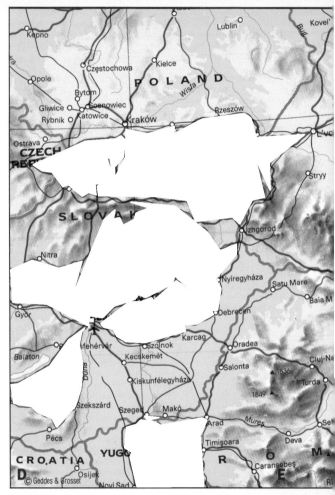

Kapno

Lublin

Kovel'

Opole

Częstochowa

Kielce

P O L A N D

Bytom

Gliwice

Sosnowiec

Rzeszów

Rybnik

Katowice

Kraków

Wisła

Ostrava

L'vc

CZECH
REP

Stryy

S L O V A K

Uzhgorod

Nitra

Nyíregyháza

Satu Mare

Győr

Debrecen

Baia M

Balaton

Karcag

Oradea

sfehérvár

Szolnok

Kecskemét

Salonta

Cluj-Na

Kiskunfélegyháza

1836

Turda

1849

Szekszárd

Szeged

Makó

Arad

Mureș

Se

Pécs

Timişoara

Deva

M

CROATIA

YUGO

R

Caransebeş

© Geddes & Grosset

Osijek

Novi Sad

O

E

Ri

D

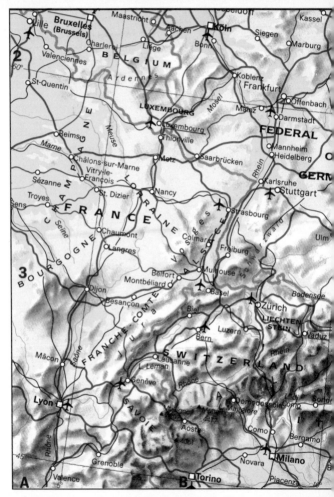

A 25° 20° Grimsey **B** 15° **C** Arctic Circle

Ísafjördhur

Húna-
flói ○Húsavik

▲845 ○Akureyri

Blönduós ○Seydhisfjördhur

I C E L A N D 70°

65° 65°

Faxaflói ▲1765 ▲1833

25° Vatnajökull Höfn○

Reykjavík 15°

Kópavogur 2119▲ ○

Keflavík Hella ○

ICELAND
Same scale

Vestmannaeyjar
•Surtsey 20°

Lofoten Vesterålen

Hinnöy

Vestfjorden

Bodö○

Same scale 7° 10°

Streymoy ------ Arctic Circle ------

○Tórshavn 62°

Faroe Is. Sandoy

Suduroy

FØROYAR
(FAEROES)
(Denmark) 7°

65°

5°

N O R W E G I A N

O

Grong○

1390▲ Hoting○

Steinkjer **S**

S E A Strömsund○

Trondheim Trondhei-
msf. Storlien○ Östersund○

Molde○ Storsjön Bräcke○

Stören○

Ålesund○ 1716▲

Oppdal○ Femunden

2286▲

© Geddes & Grosset Dombås

3

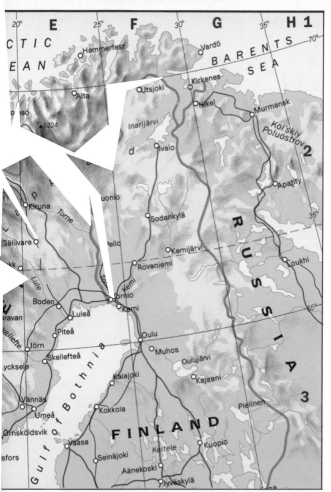

E   F   G   H 1

20°   25°   30°   35°   70°

CTIC   Hammerfest   Vardö   BARENTS   SEA

EAN   Alta   Utsjoki   Kirkenes

o Iso   ▲1324   Inarijärvi   Nikel   Murmansk

d   Ivalo   Kol'skiy Poluostrov   2

Apatity   35°

Kiruna   uonio   Sodankylä   R   U

Torne   Pello   Kemijärvi   S   Loukhi

Gällivare   Rovaniemi   S

kk   Kemi   55°   I

Boden   Tornio   A

ravan   Luleå   Kemi

Piteå   Oulu   3

Jörn   Muhos   Oulujärvi

Skellefteå   Kalajoki   Kajaani

ycksele   Gulf of Bothnia   Pielinen

Vännäs   Kokkola

Umeå   FINLAND

Örnsköldsvik   Vaasa   Keitele   Kuopio

sfors   Seinäjoki   Äänekoski   Jyväskylä

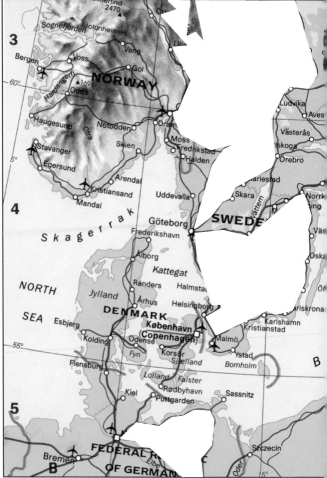

Sognefjorden Jotunheimen 2470
Vang
Bergen Voss
Gol
Hardangerfj. NORWAY
160
Oddá
60°
Haugesund Notodden Dram
Moss
Stavanger Skien Fredrikstad
Egersund Halden
Arendal
Kristiansand Uddevalla
Mandal
Göteborg SWEDE
Skagerrak Frederikshavn
Ålborg
Kattegat
NORTH Jylland Randers Halmstad
Århus Helsingborg
SEA Esbjerg DENMARK
Kolding København
Odense (Copenhagen) Malmö
Fyn Korsør Kristianstad
Flensburg Sjælland Ystad
Lolland Falster Bornholm
Kiel Rødbyhavn Sassnitz
Puttgarden
Ludvika
Aves
Västerås
rlskoga
Örebro
Mariestad
Skara Norrk
ping
Vät
Oska
rlskrona
Karlshamn
B
Szczecin
FEDERAL R
Bremen Elbe
B OF GERMAN
Oder
15°
Skarak
Oslo
Lille

Parkano
Jämsänkoski
Pori
Pere
Päijänne
Rauma
Lahti
Åland
(Ahvenanmaa)
rku   Salo
Ilo
Kotka
Espoo
Helsingfors
Gulf of Finland
Sankt
(Helsinki)
Peterburg
Norrtälje
Tallinn
Narva
ckholm
je
Luga
Hiiumaa
ESTONIA
Chudskoye
Ozero
RUSS
Saaremaa
Pärnu
Pskov
S
E
A
by
Gulf of
Gotland
Riga
LATVIA
Riga
I
C
Liepāja
LIT
Nem
Gulf of
RUSSIA
Danzig
Gdynia
Kaliningrad
nsk
5
P
ND
E

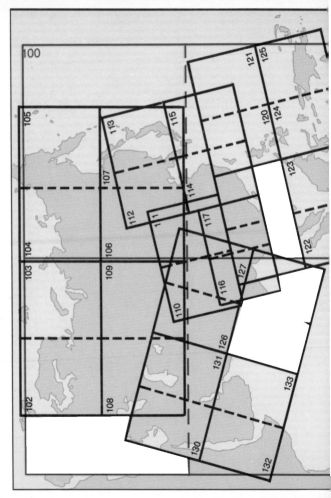

98-99   ASIA POLITICAL (W)

100-101   ASIA POLITICAL (E)

102-103   RUSSIA (N.W.)

104-105   RUSSIA (N.E.)

106-107   RUSSIA (S.E.)

108-109   RUSSIA (S.W.)

110-111   EASTERN ASIA (N.W.)

112-113   EASTERN ASIA (N.E.)

114-115   EASTERN ASIA (S.E.),
             CENTRAL JAPAN

116-117   EASTERN ASIA (S.W.)

118-119   S.E. ASIA (W)

120-121   S.E. ASIA (E)

122-123   MALAYSIA & INDONESIA (W)

124-125   INDONESIA (E)

126-127   NORTHERN INDIA & THE
             HIMALAYAS

128-129   SOUTHERN INDIA

130-131   MIDDLE EAST (N)

132-133   MIDDLE EAST (S)

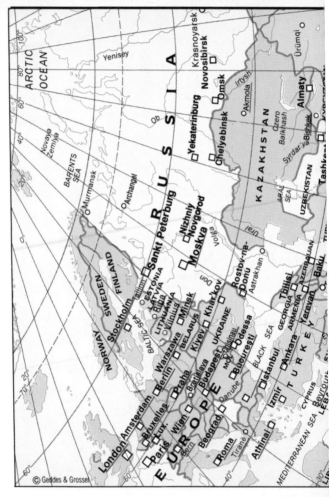

© Geddes & Grosset

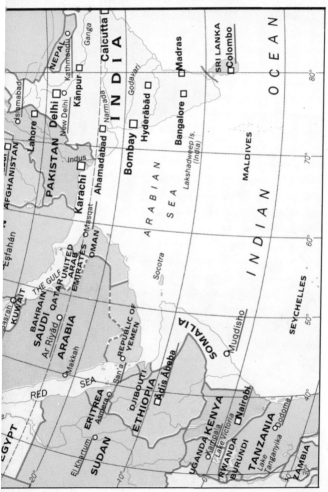

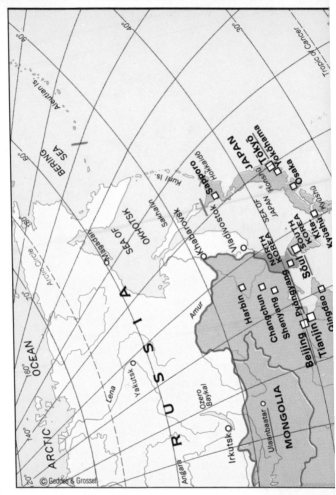

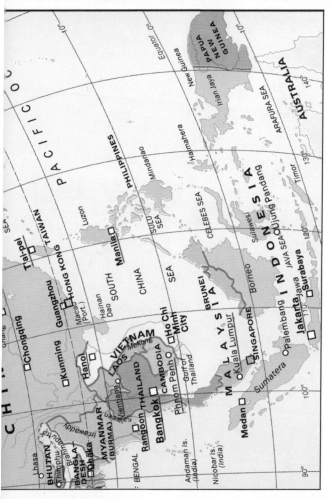

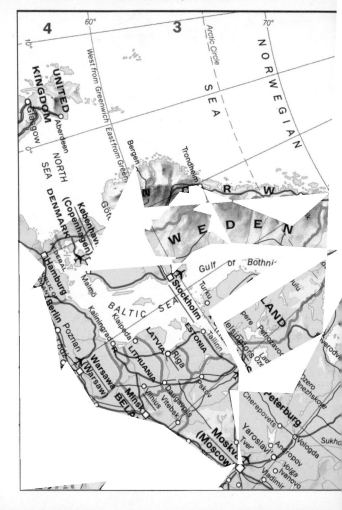

A B C

Spitsbergen

S v a l b a r d
(Norway)

Edgeøya

Nordaustlandet

ARCTIC
OCEAN

Zemlya Frantsa Iosifa

D

E

F

G

H

J

K

B A R E N T S

S E A

Novaya Zemlya

K A R A

S E A

mansk

ky

av

O. Kolguyev

P

ngel

R U S S I A

Pechora

Nar'yan Mar

O. Vaygach

Poluostrov
Yamal

Gydanskiy
Poluostrov

Ukhta

Vorkuta

Labytnangi

Ob

G. Narodnaya
1894

Uralskiy Khrebet

Obskaya Guba

Noril'sk

Yenisey

Igarka

Syktyvkar

© Geddes & Grosset

1

80°
170°
180°
150°
140°
130°
120°
110°
100°
0°

ARCTIC

OCEAN

Novosibirskiye
Ostrova

O. Komsomolets
O. Oktyabr'skoy
Revolyutsii
Severnaya Zemlya
O. Bol'shevik

O. Faddeyevskiy
O. Novaya Sibir
O. Bol'shoy
Lyakhovskiy

EAST

L   M   N   O   P   Q   R   S   T   U

LAPTEV
SEA

O. Kotel'nyy

Gory Byrranga

Ozero
Taymyr

p o l u o s t r o v
T a y m y r

Lena

Khrebet Orulgan

R U S S I A

Gory
Putorana

R U S S I A

Verkhoyansk

S r e d n e

Yakutsk

© Geddes & Grosset.

3   4

CHUKCHI
SEA

O. Vrangelya

Arctic Circle

Chukotskiy Khrebet · Chukotskiy Poluostrov

St. Lawrence
I. (U.S.A.)

B E R I N G   S E A

Kolyma

Khrebet Kolymskiy

Koryakskiy Khrebet

Zaliv
Shelikhova

Cherskogo

Magadan

Ust'-Kamchatsk

K a m c h a t k a

Sredinnyy Khrebet

Klyuchevskaya Sopka
4750

Petropavlovsk-Kamchatskiy

S E A   O F

O K H O T S K

Ozhugdzhur

va

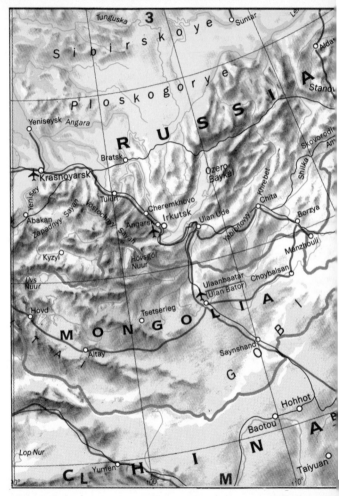

Khrebet

4

Aleksandrovsk-
Sakhalinskiy

Sakhalin

5

Ost

Kuril'skiye

(Kuril Is.)

Khrebet

Amur

Komsomolsk
ona-Amure

150

Sovetskaya
Gavan

Belogorsk

Blagoveshchensk

Birobidzhan

Khabarovsk

Yuzhno-Sakhalinsk

Xiao Hinggan Ling

Ussuri

Wakkanai

Hokkaidō

Sapporo

40

Qiqihar

Oz. Khanka

Sikhote-Alin

Ussuriysk

Hakodate

Aomori

Harbin

Vladivostok

Nakhodka

S E A   O F

Sendai

Jilin

Ch'ŏngjin

J A P A N

Niigata

Changchun

Fushun

**NORTH
KOREA**

40

JAPAN

Tōkyō

6

Shenyang

Anshan

Hamhŭng

Honshū

Yokohama

Kyōto

Nagoya

Jinzhou

Wŏnsan

**SOUTH
KOREA**

Kōbe

Ōsaka

Lüda

P'yŏngyang

**Sŏul
(Seoul)**

Taegu

Bo Hai

Taejŏn

Pusan

n

Huang

iazhuang

Qingdao

Kwangju

Mokp'o

YELLOW

SEA

Kita

Shikoku

Fukuoka

Kyūshū

Kyūshū

30

Jinan

Huang

Kagoshima

O

© Geddes & Grosset

130°

P

120°

N

7

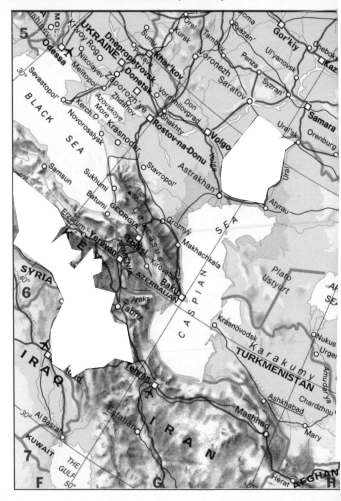

Z a p a d n o

Sergino

Perm

Serov

Surgut

Ob

stinov

Nizhniy Tagil

S i b i r s k a y a

Ural'skiy

Zlatoust

Tyumen

Tobol'sk

Irtysh

R U S S I A

gorsk

Chelyabinsk

Petropavlovsk

Omsk

n n o s t

Tobol

Ishim

Novosibirsk

Tomsk

Prok

K A Z A K H S T A N

Akmola

Pavlodar

Barnaul

Ob

Irtysh

Semipalatinsk

Karaganda

Kzyl Orda

Balkhash

Syrdar'ya

Ozero
Balkhash

lkum

Aulie At

Chimkent

Tash

STAN

H   N

gi

-154

C H I N A

Tarim

Tarim   Pendi

80°

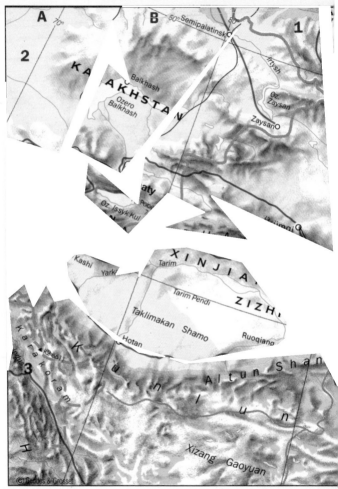

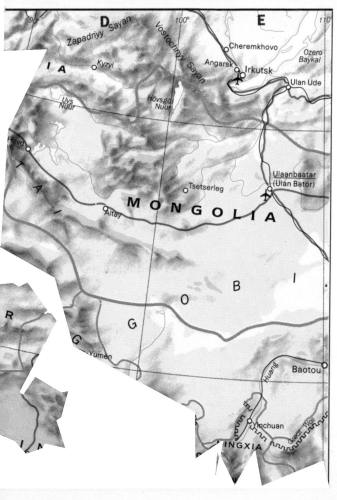

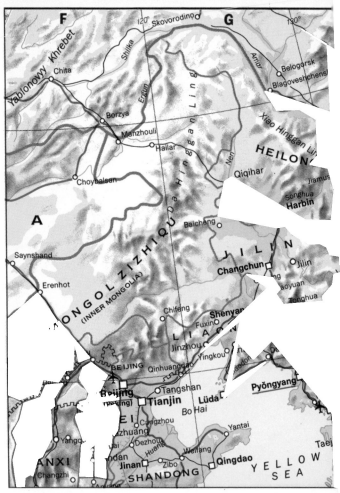

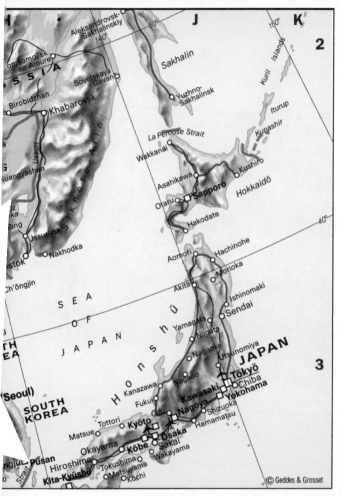

H   J   150°   K   2

Aleksandrovsk-
Sakhalinskiy
140°   50°
omsomol'sk
na-Amure
RUSSIA   Sakhalin   Kuril Islands
Birobidzhan
Khabarovsk   Sovetskaya
Gavan   Yuzhno-
Sakhalinsk   Iturup
Kuangyashan   Kunashir
La Perouse Strait
Wakkanai
Ussuri   Asahikawa   Kushiro
Sikhote Alin   Otaru   Sapporo   Hokkaidō
 Nakhodka   Hakodate   40°
ostok
Ussurysk   Aomori   Hachinohe
Ch'ŏngjin   Morioka
Akita
SEA   Ishinomaki
Honshū   Sendai
OF   Yamagata
JAPAN   Niigata
Nagaoka
Utsunomiya   JAPAN
(Seoul)   Nagano   Tōkyō   3
Kanazawa   Kawasaki   Chiba
SOUTH   Fukui   Gifu   Yokohama
KOREA   Nagoya   Shizuoka
Matsue   Tottori   Hamamatsu
Kyōto
Okayama   Osaka
ngju Pusan   Kōbe   Sakai
Hiroshima   Wakayama
Strait   Tokushima
Kita-Kyūshū   OMatsuyama
Kōchi   © Geddes & Grosset

Linfen
Xinxiang
Jining
Lianyungang
Sanmenxia
Zhengzhou
Xuzhou
Cheju do
Luoyang
Kaifeng
JIANGSU
HENAN
Xuchang
Qingjiang
Nanyang
Luohe
Bengbu
Huainan
Yangzhou
Nantong
Huai
Xinyang
Nanjing
Wuxi
Lu'an
Zhenjiang
Shanghai
Hangzhou
E A
Shashi
Shaoxing
Ningbo
CH
ngting
Hu
ZHEJIANG
S
Yiyang
ngdezhen
Jinhua
Qu Xian
Yua
Shangrao
Wenzhou
HU
Fuzhou
Shaoyang
Nanping
C
A FUJIAN
Fuzhou
Chen Xian
Chi-lung
Guilin
Sh
T'ai-pei
Xiamen
TAIWAN
Wuzhou
GU
Chang-hua
Xi
Shantou
Tái-nan
Kao-hsiung
Foshan
Guangzhou
Kowloon
Macau
Victoria
(Macao)
HONG KONG
Maoming
(Port.)
Batan Is.
Zhanjiang
Luzon Strait
Babuyan Is.
Haikou
SOUTH
CHINA
Hainan
Dao
SEA
C. Eng
Laoag
Aparri
0° © Geddes & Grosset
F
PHILIPPINES
120°
Luzon
G

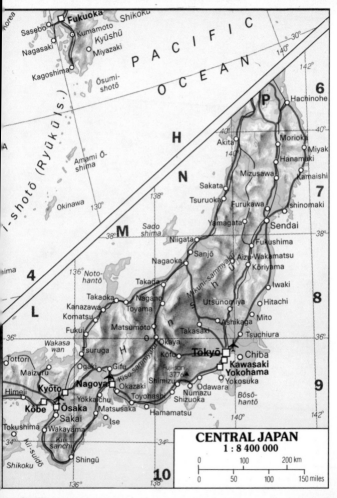

CENTRAL JAPAN
1 : 8 400 000

| 0 | | 100 | | 200 km |
| 0 | 50 | | 100 | 150 miles |

© Geddes & Grosset

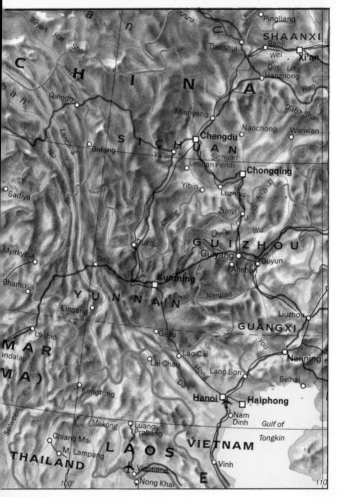

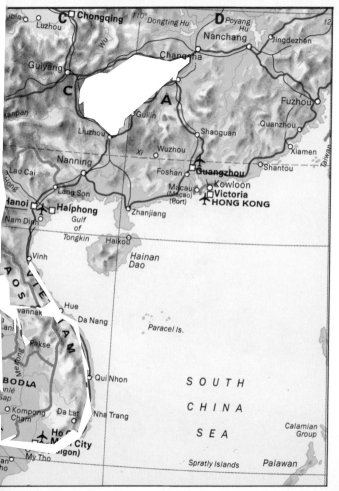

Yibin
Luzhou
C □**Chongqing**   110°   Dongting Hu   **D**   Poyang Hu   12
Nanchang   Jingdezhen
Changsha
Guiyang
C   A   Fuzhou
Guilin   Quanzhou
anpan   Liuzhou   Shaoguan   Xiamen
Xi   Wuzhou
Nanning   Foshan   □**Guangzhou**   Shantou
Lao Cai   Taiwan
ong   Macau   Kowloon
Lang Son   (Macao)   □**Victoria**
Hanoi □   ⊐**Haiphong**   (Port)   **HONG KONG**
Nam Dinh   Gulf   Zhanjiang
of
Tongkin   Haikou
Vinh   **Hainan
Dao**
A   **VIETNAM**
O   Hue
vannak   Da Nang   *Paracel Is.*
ani
Pakse
BODIA
anlé   **S O U T H**
Sap
Kompong   Da Lat   Qui Nhon
Cham   Nha Trang   **C H I N A**
Ho C   City   Calamian
(aigon)   **S E A**   Group
an   My Tho   *Spratly Islands*   Palawan

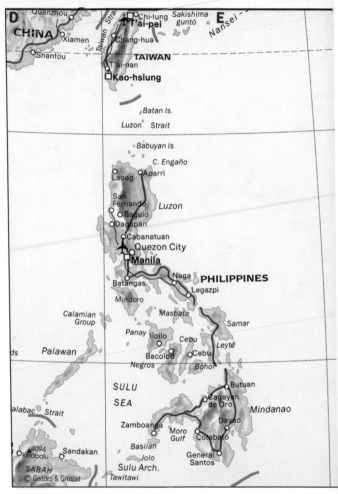

Quanzhou
CHINA
Xiamen
Shantou

D

Chi-lung
T'ai-pei
Chang-hua
TAIWAN
T'ai-nan
Kao-hsiung

Taiwan Strait

Sakishima guntó
E
Nansei –

Batan Is.
Luzon Strait

Babuyan Is

C. Engaño

Laoag
Aparri
San Fernando
Baguio
Dagupan
Cabanatuan
Quezon City
Manila
Batangas

Luzon

Naga **PHILIPPINES**
Legazpi

Mindoro
Masbate
Calamian Group
Panay Iloilo Cebu
Bacolod Cebu
Negros Bohol

Samar
Leyte

Palawan

ds

Butuan
Cagayan de Oro
Mindanao

SULU SEA

Zamboanga
Moro Gulf
Davao
Cotabato

alabac Strait

4094 Kinabalu
Sandakan

Basilan
Jolo
SABAH
© Geddes & Grosset
Sulu Arch.
Tawitawi

General Santos

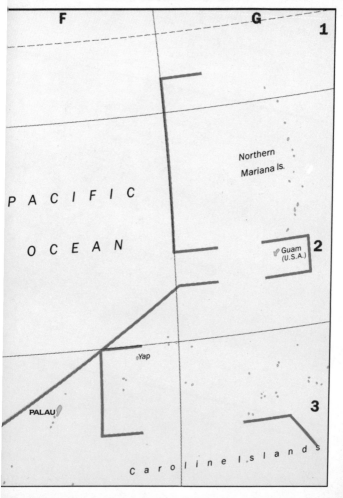

F   G   1

Northern
Mariana Is.

PACIFIC

OCEAN

Guam
(U.S.A.)   2

Yap

PALAU   3

Caroline Islands

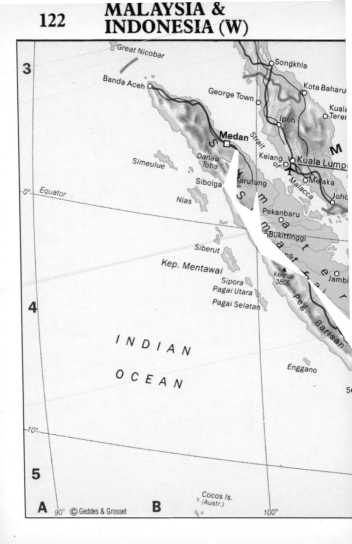

Great Nicobar

Banda Aceh

George Town

Songkhla

Kota Baharu

Kuala Teren

Ipoh

Medan

Kelang

Kuala Lumpur

M

Simeulue

Danau Toba

Strait of

Melaka

Sibolga

Tarutung

Malacca

Joho

Nias

S

Equator

Pekanbaru

Bukittinggi

Siberut

Kep. Mentawai

Sipora

Pagai Utara

Pagai Selatan

Kerinci
3805

Jambi

Peg. Barisan

INDIAN

OCEAN

Enggano

-10°

Cocos Is.
(Austr.)

A

90° © Geddes & Grosset

B

100°

3

4

5

Con
Son

Balabac   Strait

Kota
Kinabalu   ▲4094
Kinabalu   Sandakan

Bandar   SABAH
Seri Begawan
BRUNEI

L A Y S I A

Natuna
Besar

Miri

Kep. Anambas   Kep.
Natuna

Tawau

Singkawang   Sibu   Tarakan

APORE   Kuching   S A R A W A K
                                Rajang   Peg. Iran

ga   Pontianak

K A L I M A N T A N
Borneo

G. Menyapa
2000

Bangka   Samarinda

Pangkalpinang   Balikpapan

Peg. Schwaner   Palu

embang   Belitung
                    Palangkaraya   Kandangan   Makassar   Strait

                                          Banjarmasin   Majene

Tg. Puting   Laut   Parepare

I N D O N E S I A

JAVA SEA   Ujung
                                Pandang

Telukbetung

da   ✈ **Jakarta**

Bogor   Cirebon Semarang   Madura   FLORES

Bandung   Surakarta   Lesser

                ▲3428   **Surabaya**   Bali   Sunda
        Yogyakarta Kediri   Lombok   Raba
J a w a   Malang   Banyuwangi
                                        Mataram
        (J a v a)   Sumbawa   Sumba

Christmas I.
(Austr.)
                                                        D
110°
                                                        12

SULU
SEA

Butuan

Cagayan
de Oro

Zamboanga

Mindanao

PALAU

Basilan
Moro
Gulf

Davao

Cotabato

PHILIPPINES

Jolo

Sulu Arch.

General
Santos

Tawitawi

CELEBES

SEA

Kep.
Talaud

Kep.
Sangihe

Morotai

Manado

Halmahera

Gorontalo

MOLUCCA
SEA

Waigeo

Teluk

Kep. Togian

Manokw

Tomini

Poso

Kep.
Banggai

Kep. Sula

MALUKU (MOLUCCAS)

Obi

SERAM SEA

Sorong

Misoöl

Ce

Sulawesi
(Celebes)

Kendari

Buru

Seram

Fakfak

Ambon

Muna

Butung

I N D O N E S I A

Kep.
Kai

Salayar

BANDA   SEA

SEA

Yamdena

Trang

Islands

Wetar

Babar

Kepulauan
Tanimbar

Flores

Alor

Ruteng

Ende

Dili

Kep.
Leti

ARAFURA

SAWU SEA

Timor

20°

© Geddes & Grosset

Roti

Kupang

E

130°

3

C a r o l i n e   I s l a n d s

Equator   0°

Biak

Yapen

Admiralty Is.

Jayapura

Wewak

Bismarck Archipelago

BISMARCK SEA

IRIAN

Sepik

4

Pegunungan   Maoke

Pk. Jaya
5029

JAYA

Central
Range

PAPUA

Madang

Mt.
Hagen

▲4508
▲Mt Wilhelm

Lae

New Guinea

NEW GUINEA

New
Britain

Wau

D'Entrecasteaux
Is.

Fly

Owen Stanley Range

P. Dolak

rg. Vals

Merauke

Daru

Port Moresby

10°

Alotau

5

Torres   Strait
C. York

AUSTRALIA   CORAL SEA

G

140°

H

150°

Yume

Qilian Shan

Qinghai Hu

2

Altu

Golmu

Shan

Bayan Har Shan

Jinsha

n   u   n

Lancang

Xizang   Gaoyuan

HINA   Tanggula Shan

Nu

-30°

Nam Co

se Sh

Lhasa

Sadiya

Dibrugarh

maputra

Naga Hills   3

Myitkyina

npur

cknow

Gorakhpur   Rangpur   Shillong

ur   Mymensingh   Imphal   MYANMAR
(BURMA)

bād   BANGLADESH

Mirzapur   Dhāka
(Dacca)   Tropic of Cancer

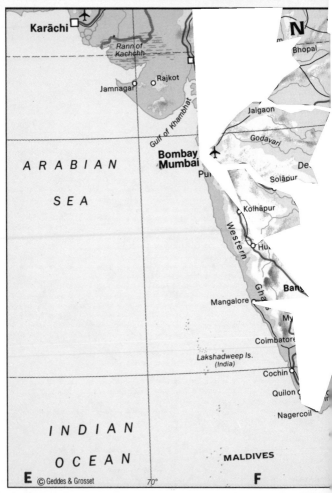

Karāchi

Rann of Kachchh

Jamnagar   Rajkot

Gulf of Khambhat

N

Bhopal

Jalgaon

Godavari

Bombay Mumbai

Pu

De

Solāpur

A R A B I A N

S E A

Kolhāpur

Western

Hu

Ghats

Ban

Mangalore

My

Coimbatore

Lakshadweep Is.
(India)

Cochin

Quilon

Nagercoil

I N D I A N

O C E A N

E © Geddes & Grosset   70°   **MALDIVES**   **F**

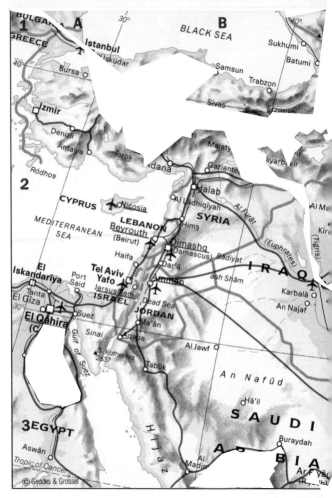

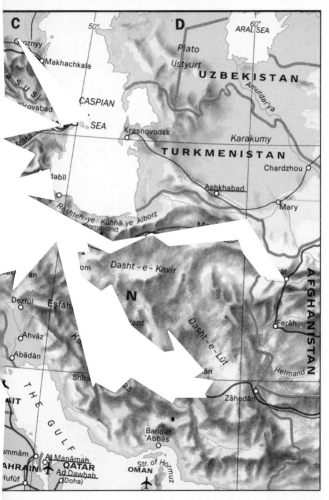

C 50° D 60°
ARAL SEA

Groznyy
Makhachkala

Plato
Ustyurt

UZBEKISTAN

CASPIAN

Amudar'ya

Kirovabad

SEA

Krasnovodsk

Karakumy

TURKMENISTAN

Chardzhou

Araks

Nabīl

Ashkhabad

Mary

Rashteh-ye Kūhhā ye Alborz
Damavand

Qom

Dasht - e - Kavir

M

AFGHANISTAN

N

Dezfūl

Esfahān

Yazd

Dasht - e - Lūt

Farāh

Ahvāz

Kō

Abādān

Shīrā

Helmand

Zāhedān

THE

Bandar
'Abbās

AIT

GULF

mmām

Al Manāmah

QATAR

Str. of Hormuz

OMAN

AHRAIN

Ad Dawhah

ufūf

(Doha)

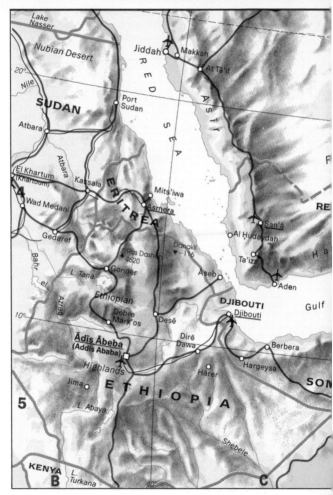

Lake Nasser

Nubian Desert

Jiddah

Makkah

At Tā'if

20°

Nile

SUDAN

'Asīr

RED SEA

Atbara

Port Sudan

El Khartum
(Khartoum)

Atbara

Kassala

ERITREA

Mits'iwa

Asmera

San'ā

Wad Medani

Al Ḥudaydah

Gedaref

Ras Dashan
4620

Danakil
▼ -116

Ta'izz

Aden

Bahr el

L. Tana

Gonder

Aseb

Azraq

Ethiopian

10°

Debre Mark'os

Desē

Dirē Dawa

DJIBOUTI
Djibouti

Gulf

Berbera

Ādīs Ābeba
(Addis Ababa)

Highlands

Hārer

Hargeysa

SOM

Jima

ETHIOPIA

5

L. Abaya

Shebele

KENYA

L. Turkana

B   40°   C

RE

F

Ha

S

RE

Abū Zabī
(Abu Dhabi)   Dubayy   Gulf of Oman

UNITED
ARAB
EMIRATES   Al Khābūrah   Masqat
(Muscat)

Ra's al Hadd

OMAN

al   Kn ā l ī   Maşīrah

al   **ARABIAN**

OF YEMEN   Şalālah   **SEA**

m ā u t

Al Mukallā

Socotra
(Suqutra)
(Rep. of Yemen)

INDIAN   OCEAN

50°   **D**   60°   © Geddes & Grosset

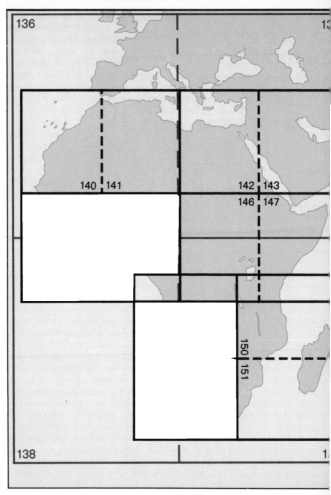

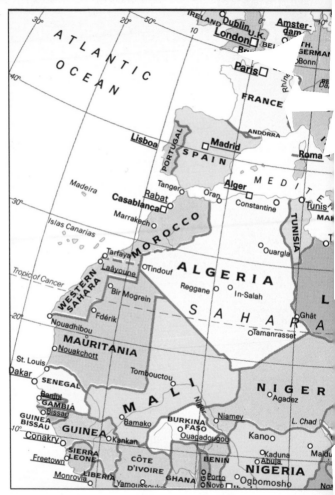

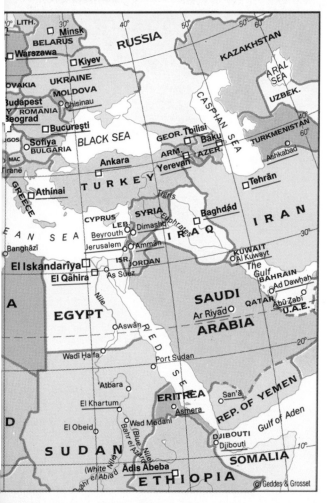

LITH. 30° 40° 50° 50° 60°

☐ Minsk

BELARUS

☐ Warszawa RUSSIA KAZAKHSTAN

☐ Kiev

OVAKIA UKRAINE ARAL SEA

MOLDOVA

Budapest O Chisinau UZBEK.

Y ROMANIA

Beograd

☐ Bucureşti CASPIAN SEA 40°

UGOS. O Sofiya BLACK SEA GEOR. Tbilisi 60° TURKMENISTAN

BULGARIA ARM. ☐ Baku

MAC Ankara AZER. Ashkabad O

Tirane Yerevan

GREECE T U R K E Y ☐ Tehrān

☐ Athínai

CYPRUS SYRIA Baghdād I R A N

LEB. Euphrates

E A N   S E A Beyrouth O Dimashq ☐ 30°

Banghāzī Jerusalem O Ammān I R A Q KUWAIT

ISR. O Al Kuwayt

El Iskandariya ☐ JORDAN The Gulf BAHRAIN

El Qāhira As Suez Ad Dawhah O

SAUDI QATAR Abū Zabi

A Nile Ar Riyād O U.A.E.

EGYPT ARABIA

O Aswān 20°

Wadī Halfa O RED Port Sudan O SEA

Atbara O

El Khartum O ERITREA O San'ā

Asmera O REP. OF YEMEN

El Obeid O O Wad Medani Gulf of Aden

(Blue Nile) DJIBOUTI

(White) Nile O Djibouti 10°

S U D A N Ādis Ābeba ☐ SOMALIA

(Bahr el Azraq) E T H I O P I A

(Bahr el Abiad) © Geddes & Grosset

D

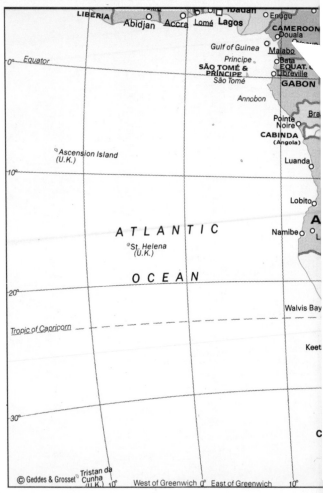

LIBERIA

Abidjan   Accra   Lomé   **Lagos**   Ibadan   Enugu

CAMEROON
Douala

Gulf of Guinea   Malabo

Principe   Bata

SÃO TOMÉ & PRÍNCIPE   Libreville

São Tomé   **EQUAT.**

GABON

0°   *Equator*

Annobon

Bra

Pointe Noire

CABINDA
(Angola)

Luanda

Ascension Island
(U.K.)

10°

Lobito

A

Namibe

A T L A N T I C

St. Helena
(U.K.)

O C E A N

20°

Walvis Bay

Tropic of Capricorn

Keet

30°

C

© Geddes & Grosset   Tristan da Cunha
(U.K.)   10°   West of Greenwich   0°   East of Greenwich   10°

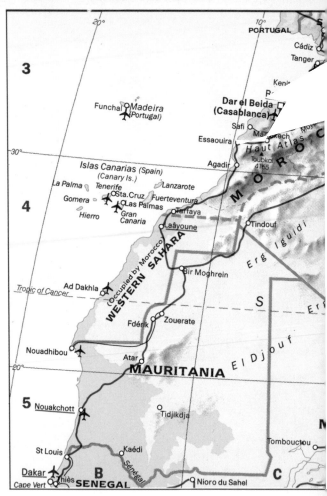

PORTUGAL

3

Cádiz
Tanger
Keni·
Dar el Beida
(Casablanca)
Funchal ○ Madeira
(Portugal)
Safi
Essaouira   Marrakech   Moy
Haut Atlas
30°
Agadir
Islas Canarias (Spain)
(Canary Is.)
La Palma   Tenerife   Lanzarote
4   Gomera   Sta.Cruz   Fuerteventura
Hierro   Las Palmas
Gran   Tarfaya
Canaria
Laâyoune   Tindouf
I g u i d i
Erg
Bir Moghrein
S
Tropic of Cancer   Ad Dakhla
(Occupied by Morocco)
Err
WESTERN SAHARA
Fdérik   Zouerate
Nouadhibou   *El Djouf*
Atar
20°   **MAURITANIA**
5   Nouakchott
Tidjikdja
St Louis   Kaédi
Tombouctou
Dakar   *Sénégal*   **N**
Cape Vert   Thiès   **B**   **SENEGAL**   Nioro du Sahel   **C**

Toubkal
4165

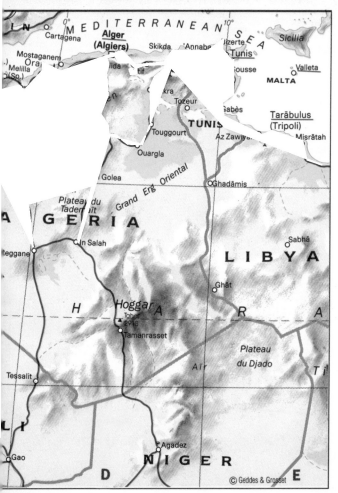

MEDITERRANEAN SEA

Cartagena

Alger (Algiers)

Skikda   Annaba   Bizerte   **Tunis**

Sicilia

Mostaganem   Oran

Melilla (Sp.)

Blida   tif

Sousse

Valleta

MALTA

kra

Tozeur

Gabès

Tunis

Touggourt

Az Zawiya

Tarābulus (Tripoli)

Misrātah

Ouargla

Golea

Grand Erg Oriental

Ghadāmis

Plateau du Tademaït

GERIA

In Salah

Sabhā

LIBYA

Reggane

Ghāt

H

Hoggar

A

Tahat 2918

Tamanrasset

R

A

Tessalit

Air

Plateau du Djado

Ti

LI

Gao

Agadez

NIGER

D

E

© Geddes & Grosset

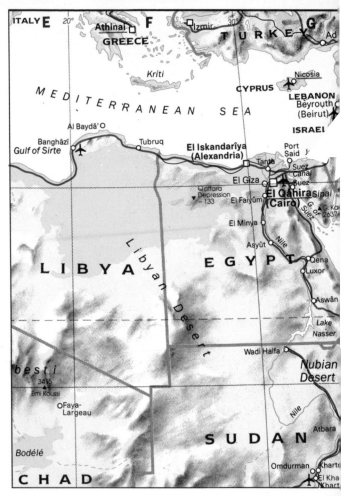

ITALY E 20° Athinai **F** Izmir 30° **TURKEY G** Ad

GREECE

Krìti

Nicosia

CYPRUS

LEBANON
Beyrouth
(Beirut)

MEDITERRANEAN SEA

ISRAEL

Al Baydã'O

Banghãzi

Gulf of Sirte

Tubruq

**El Iskandarîya
(Alexandria)**

Tanta

Port
Said

Suez
Canal

Suez

El Gîza

**El Qâhira
(Cairo)**

Sinai

G. of
Suez

G. Ka
2637

Qattara
Depression
▼ −133

El Faiyûm

El Minya

Nile

LIBYA

Libyan Desert

Asyût

EGYPT

Qena

Luxor

Aswân

Lake
Nasser

Wadi Halfa

**Nubian
Desert**

bes *t i*

3415
▲
Emi Koussi

OFaya-
Largeau

Nile

Bodélé

SUDAN

Atbara

Khartc

Omdurman

El Kha
Khart

CHAD

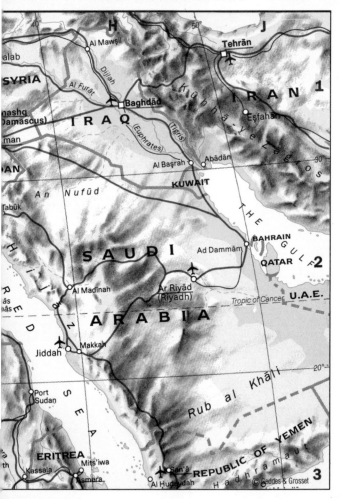

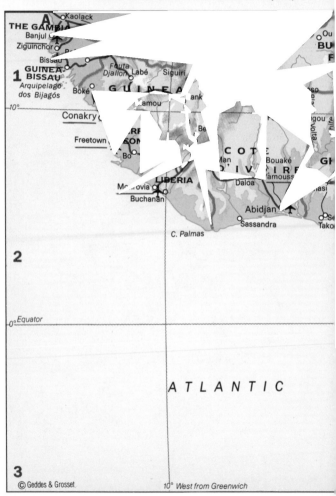

Zinder

L. Chad

E

I

Nguru

Maiduguri

Sokoto

Niger

Kaduna

Parakou

Mar

NIGERIA

Minna

Abuja

Benue

osho

da

Ilorin

Oshogbo

kuta

Benin
City

sif de L'

rdi

Niger

Porto
Novo

Lagos

Port
Harcourt

CAMEROON

Nkongsamba

cra

Bight of Benin

Cameoun
4095▲

ouala

Yaoundé

Malabo

Bioko

GULF OF GUINEA

EQUATORIAL

Príncipe GUINEA

SÃO TOMÉ &
PRÍNCIPE

São Tomé

Bata

Oyem

Sangha

Libreville

Port Gentil

Lambaréné

CONGO

GABON

Annobón
(Equat. Guinea)

Franceville

Gamboma

Congo

CEAN

Brazzaville

Pointe Noire

Kinshasa

Kwango

CABINDA
(Angola)

Boma

Matadi

ANGOLA

10° East from Greenwich

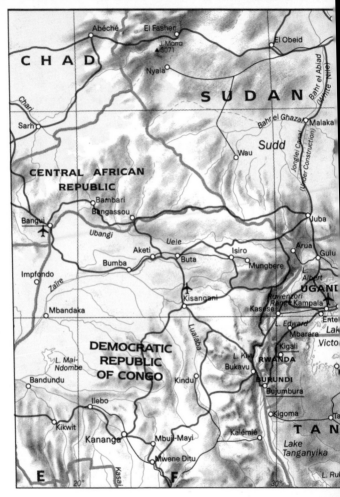

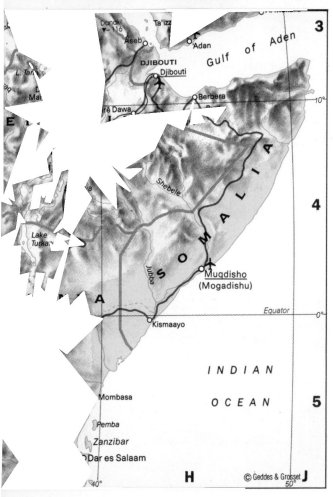

Dānākil
▼-116
Ta'izz
Aseb
'Adan
Gulf of Aden **3**
DJIBOUTI
Djibouti
Berbera
Dawa
10°
S
O
M
A
L
I
A **4**
Shebele
L. Tana
Mai
E
Lake
Turkana
Jubba
Muqdisho
(Mogadishu)
Equator **0°**
Kismaayo
A
INDIAN
OCEAN **5**
Mombasa
Pemba
Zanzibar
Dar es Salaam
40°
H
© Geddes & Grosset
50°
J

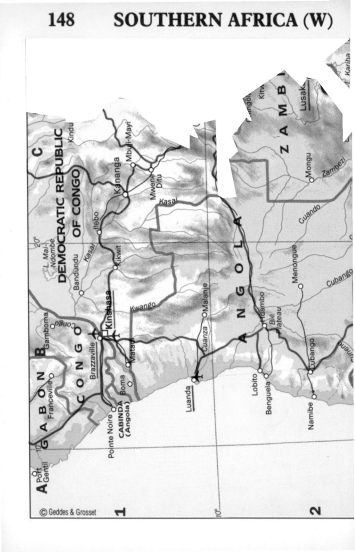

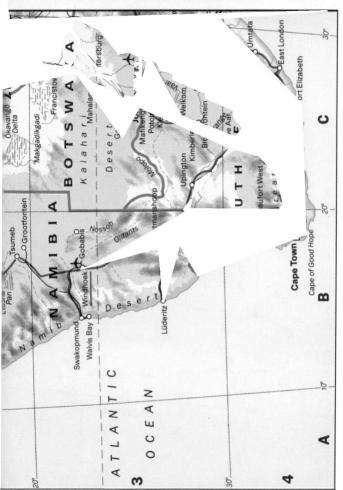

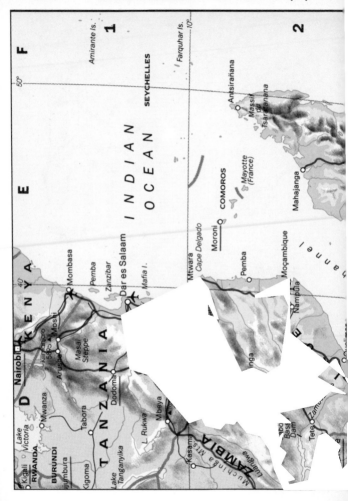

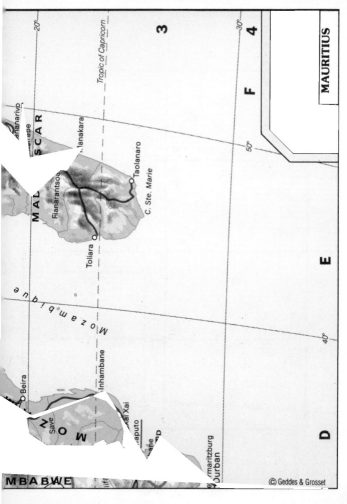

MAURITIUS

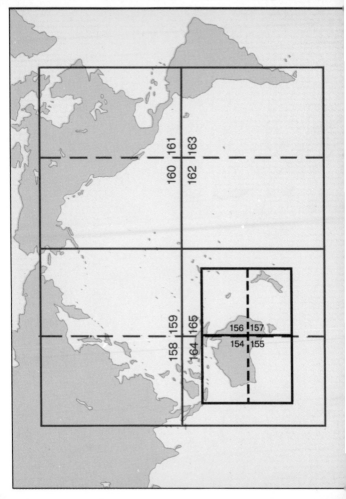

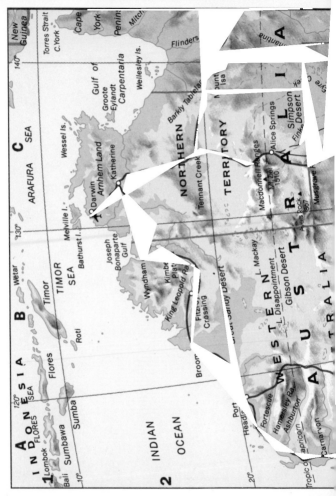

New Guinea

Torres Strait
C. York
Cape York Penin.
Flinders
Mitch
anunu

140°

Gulf of
Carpentaria
Groote Eylandt
Wellesley Is.
Barkly Tableland

A

L

I

A

Eyre Cr

Mount
Isa

Simpson Desert
Finke

Alice Springs

Macdonnell Ranges
Mt
1510

R

Musgrave

Avers Rock
867

NORTHERN TERRITORY

Tennant Creek

Wessel Is.

SEA

C

ARAFURA

Darwin
Arnhem Land
Katherine

Melville I.
Bathurst I.

130°

Joseph Bonaparte Gulf

Wyndham

Kimb
Plat
King Leopold Ra.

Fitzroy Crossing

L. Mackay

L. Disappointment

Gibson Desert

W E S T E R N

A U S T R A L I A

Great Sandy Desert

Broom

Port

Forrest

Hamersley Ra.
Ashburton

Capricorn
Carnarvon

Head

Wetar

Timor

TIMOR SEA

Roti

Sumba

Sumbawa

Flores

FLORES SEA

Lombok

Bali

B

A

I

S

E

N

O

D

N

I

120°

10°

INDIAN OCEAN

2

20°

Tropic of Capricorn

1

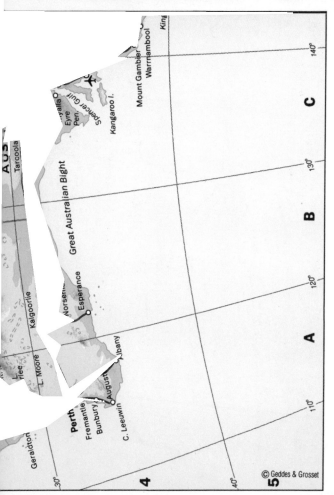

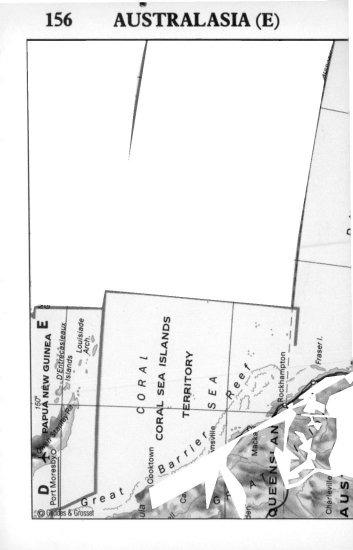

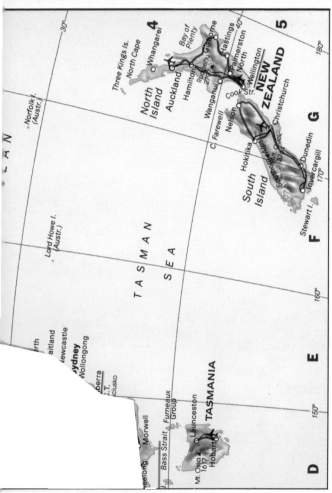

30°

Three Kings Is.
North Cape
Whangarei

Norfolk I.
(Austr.)

4

Bay of
Plenty

Gisborne

40°

5

Hastings
Palmerston
North

Ruapehu
2797

Hamilton

180°

Auckland

North
Island

**NEW
ZEALAND**

Wellington

Wanganui

Cook Str.

C. Farewell

Nelson

Christchurch

G

Mt Cook
3764

Dunedin

Hokitika

Southern Alps

170°

Invercargill

South
Island

Stewart I.

F

Lord Howe I.
(Austr.)

T A S M A N

S E A

160°

A N

L A N

...rth
...itland
Newcastle
Sydney
Wollongong
...erra
...C.T.
...iusko

E

150°

Bass Strait

Furneaux
Group

Launceston

TASMANIA

Mt Ossa
1617

Hobart

...eelong
Morwell

D

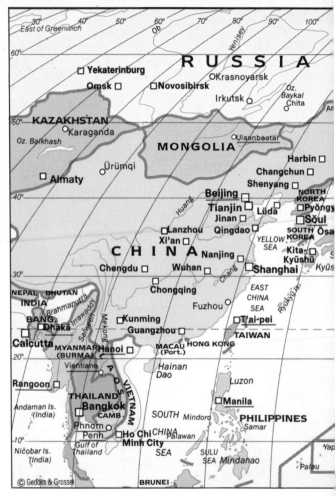

120° 130° 140° 150° 160° 170° 180° 170°

Yakutsk
Lena
St. Lawrence I.

Magadan

SEA OF
OKHOTSK

Kamchatka

Komandorskiye
Os

BERING
SEA

Aleutian Islands

Sakhalin

barovsk

Kuril Islands

vostok □Sapporo
Hokkaidō

Honshū
□Tōkyō
Yokohama
oya

P A C I F I C   O C E A N

Ogasawara-shottó
(Jap.)

Kazan-rettó
(Jap.)

Midway Is.
(U.S.A.)

Hawaiian
Islands

Northern
Mariana Is.
(U.S.A.)

Wake I.
(U.S.A.)

International Date Line

Johnston I.
(U.S.A.)

MARSHALL
ISLANDS

M i c r o n e s i a

e Islands **MICRONESIA**

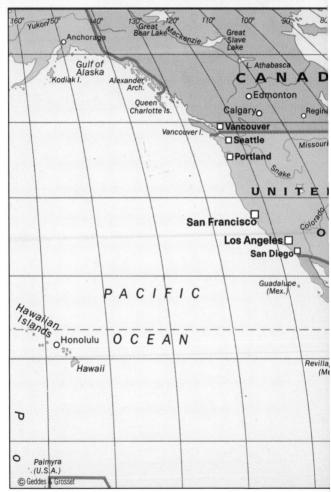

GREENLAND (Den.)
ICELAND
Reykjavik
West of Greenwich

Davis Str.

LABRADOR SEA

Newfoundland

beg

L. Superior
St. Lawrence
Montréal
Ottawa
L. Huron
L. Michigan
apolis
Detroit
Toronto
L. Ontario
Boston
Chicago
Pittsburgh
L. Erie
New York
Philadelphia
nver
Cincinnati
Baltimore
St. Louis
Ohio
Washington

AMERICA

ATLANTIC

Dallas
Atlanta

Bermuda (U.K.)

New Orleans
Mississippi

OCEAN

Houston
rande

Bravo del Nte

GULF OF
Miami
THE BAHAMAS

Monterrey
MEXICO

Tropic of Cancer

La Habana
CUBA

DOMINICAN REPUBLIC

Guadalajara
Greater

México
HAITI
Puerto Rico (U.S.A.)

BELIZE
JAMAICA
Antilles

Lesser Antilles

GUATEMALA
Guatemala
HONDURAS
Tegucigalpa
CARIBBEAN SEA

San Salvador
EL SALVADOR
NICARAGUA
Managua

Clipperton I. (Fr.)
COSTA RICA
San José
Panamá
Caracas

PANAMA
VENEZUELA

de Coco (C.R.)
Medellín

Bogotá

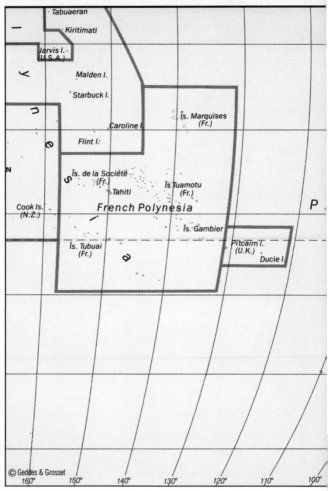

COLOMBIA

Equator   □ **Quito**   0°
                            □ **Guayaquil**
Islas Galápagos
(Ecuador)   **ECUADOR**   *Amazonas*

                                              BRAZIL

                    Trujillo ○
                            PERU   10°

                    Callao ○ □ **Lima**

                                          L. Titicaca
                    Arequipa ○   ○ La Paz

F I C   O C E A N   **BOLIVIA**
                                          Sucre   20°

                                                              PAR.
                    Tropic of Capricorn
                            Antofagasta ○
 Sala-y-Gomez (Ch.)   **Asunción** ○
de Pascua
(Ch.)

                                          ○ Córdoba   30°
                            Rosario ○   **URUGUAY**
        Is. Juan Fernández **Santiago** □   ○ **Montevideo**
            (Ch.)
                                          Buenos □   □
        Concepción ○   C H I L E   **Aires**
                            ARGENTINA

                                      Bahía Blanca   40°
            Puerto Montt ○

                    P a t a g o n i a

                                                              50°
    Punta Arenas ○   *Falkland Is.*
                        (Islas Malvinas)
        Tierra del   *(U.K.)*   South Georgia
        Fuego   *(U.K.)*
 80°   70°   60°   50°   40°   30°

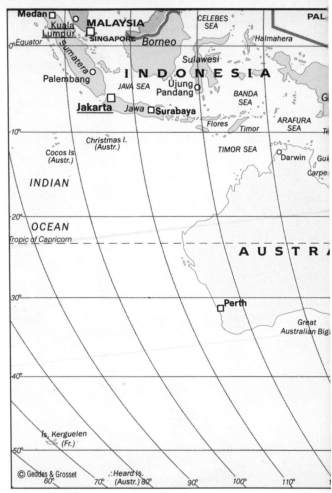

Medan

Kuala Lumpur **MALAYSIA**

SINGAPORE *Borneo*

Equator

Sumatera

Palembang

I N D O N E S I A

CELEBES SEA

Halmahera

Sulawesi

JAVA SEA Ujung Pandang

BANDA SEA

Jakarta *Jawa* □**Surabaya**

Flores Timor

ARAFURA SEA

PAL

G

-10°

Christmas I. *(Austr.)*

Cocos Is *(Austr.)*

INDIAN

TIMOR SEA

Darwin *Gui*

Carpe

-20°

OCEAN

Tropic of Capricorn

A U S T R A

-30°

□**Perth**

Great Australian Big

-40°

-50°

Is. Kerguelen *(Fr.)*

© Geddes & Grosset

60° 70° Heard Is. *(Austr.)* 80° 90° 100° 110°

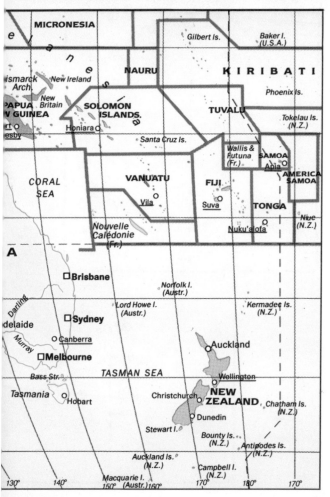

MICRONESIA

Gilbert Is.

Baker I.
(U.S.A.)

NAURU

K I R I B A T I

Bismarck Arch.

New Ireland

New Britain

Phoenix Is.

PAPUA N GUINEA

esby

SOLOMON ISLANDS

Honiara

TUVALU

Tokelau Is.
(N.Z.)

Santa Cruz Is.

Wallis & Futuna (Fr.)

SAMOA

Apia

CORAL SEA

VANUATU

FIJI

AMERICA SAMOA

Vila

Suva

TONGA

Niue
(N.Z.)

Nouvelle Calédonie
(Fr.)

Nuku'alofa

A

Brisbane

Norfolk I.
(Austr.)

Darling

Lord Howe I.
(Austr.)

Kermadec Is.
(N.Z.)

Sydney

delaide

Canberra

Auckland

Murray

Melbourne

TASMAN SEA

Wellington

Bass Str.

Christchurch

NEW ZEALAND

Chatham Is.
(N.Z.)

Tasmania

Hobart

Dunedin

Stewart I.

Bounty Is.
(N.Z.)

Auckland Is.
(N.Z.)

Antipodes Is.
(N.Z.)

Macquarie I.
(Austr.)

Campbell I.
(N.Z.)

130°   140°   150°   160°   170°   180°   170°

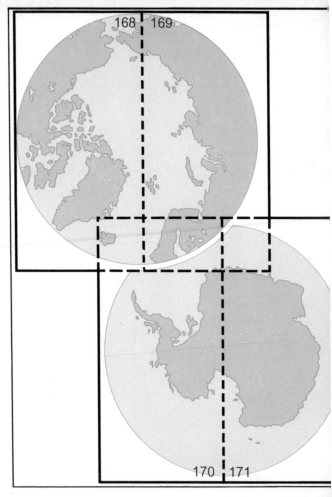

168 169

170 171

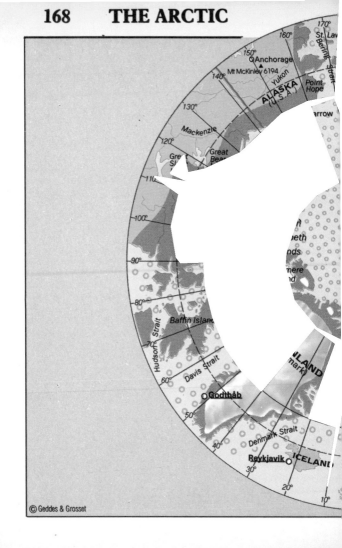

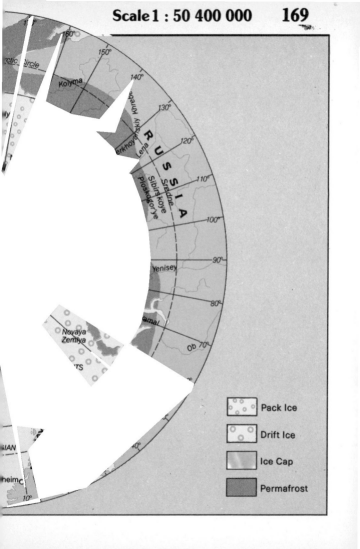

Arctic Circle

Kolyma

Verkhoyanskiy khrebet

R U S S I A

Sredne
Sibirskoye
ploskogorye

160°
150°
140°
130°
120°
110°
100°
90°
80°
70°
60°
50°
40°
30°
20°
10°

Lena

Yenisey

Yamal

Ob

Novaya
Zemlya

URAL MTS

Scandinavian?

heim

Pack Ice

Drift Ice

Ice Cap

Permafrost

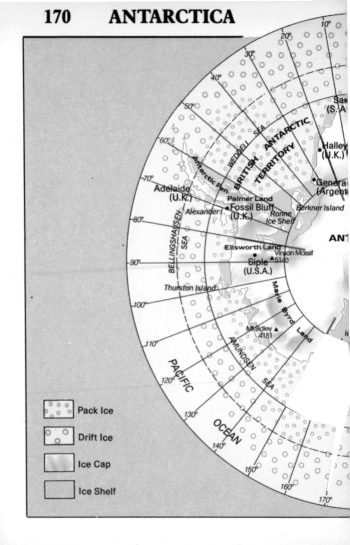

Pack Ice

Drift Ice

Ice Cap

Ice Shelf

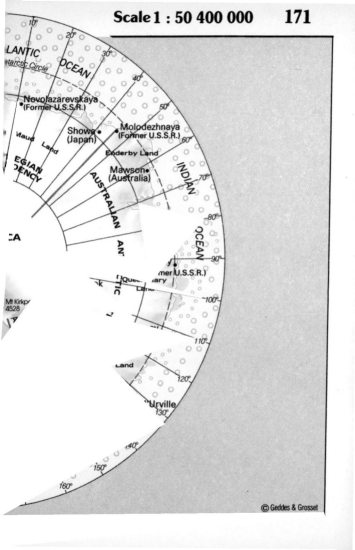

10°
20°
30°
40°
50°

ATLANTIC OCEAN
tarctic Circle

60°

Novolazarevskaya
(Former U.S.S.R.)

Showa
(Japan)

Molodezhnaya
(Former U.S.S.R.)

Maud Land

Enderby Land

EGIAN
DENCY

Mawson
(Australia)

INDIAN

70°

AUSTRALIAN

80°

:A

AN

OCEAN

90°

mer U.S.S.R.)

Mt Kirkp
4528

Quee ary

Land

100°

IC

110°

Land

120°

Urville

130°

140°

150°

160°

© Geddes & Grosset

Index

In the index, the first number refers to the page, and the following letter
and number to the section of the map in which the index entry
can be found. For example London 56G6 means that London can
be found on page 56 where column G and row 6 meet.

Abbreviations used in the Index

Afghan	Afghanistan	Fin	Finland	Phil	Phillipines
Alb	Albania	Hung	Hungary	Pol	Poland
Alg	Algeria	Indon	Indonesia	Port	Portugal
Arg	Argentina	Lat	Latvia	Rep Yemen	Republic of Yemen
Aust	Australia	Leb	Lebanon	Rom	Romania
Bang	Bangladesh	Lib	Liberia	S Africa	South Africa
Belg	Belgium	Liech	Liechtenstein	S Arabia	Saudi Arabia
Bol	Bolivia	Lith	Lithuania	S Korea	South Korea
Bos Herz	Bosnia Herzegovina	Lux	Luxembourg	Scot	Scotland
Bulg	Bulgaria	Madag	Madagascar	Sen	Senegal
Camb	Cambodia	Malay	Malaysia	Slo	Slovenia
Can	Canada	Maur	Mauritania	Switz	Switzerland
CAR	Central African Republic	Mor	Morocco	Tanz	Tanzania
Cro	Croatia	Mozam	Mozambique	Thai	Thailand
Czech Rep	Czech Republic	N Ire	Northern Ireland	Turk	Turkey
Dem Rep of Congo	Democratic Republic of Congo	N Korea	North Korea	UAE	United Arab Emirates
		NZ	New Zealand	UK	United Kingdom
Den	Denmark	Neth	Netherlands	USA	United States of America
Dom Rep	Dominican Republic	Nic	Nicaragua	Urug	Uruguay
El Sal	El Salvador	Nig	Nigeria	Ven	Venezuela
Eng	England	Nor	Norway	Viet	Vietnam
Eq Guinea	Equatorial Guinea	PNG	Papua New Guinea	Yugos	Yugoslavia
Est	Estonia	Pak	Pakistan	Zim	Zimbabwe
Eth	Ethiopia	Par	Paraguay		
FRG	Federal Republic of Germany				

A

Aachen *FRG*	90B2	Agadir *Mor*	140C3	Albuquerque *USA*	17C2
Aänekoski *Fin*	93F3	Agen *France*	69C3	Albury *Aust*	157D4
Abādān *Iran*	131C2	Agra *India*	126F3	Alcalá de Henares	
Abadla *Alg*	141C3	Agrigento *Italy*	79C3	Spain	72B1
Abakan *Rus*	106L4	Agropoli *Italy*	79C2	Alcañiz *Spain*	74B1
Abbeville *France*	68C1	Aguascalientes *Mexico*	23C3	Alcàzar de San Juan	
Abéché *Chad*	146F3	Ahmadābād *India*	128F3	Spain	73B2
Abeokuta *Nig*	145D2	Ahvāz *Iran*	131C2	Alcoy *Spain*	75B2
Aberdeen *Scot*	61F3	Aīn Sefra *Alg*	141C3	Aldan *Russia*	106O4
Aberfeldy *Scot*	63E4	Aizu-Wakamatsu *Japan*	115N8	Alderney I. *UK*	59E8
Abergavenney *Wales*	58D6	Ajaccio *Corse*	76B2	Aldershot *Eng*	56G6
Abersoch *Wales*	53C5	Ajmer *India*	126F3	Aleksandrovsk-Sakhalinsky	
Aberystwyth *Wales*	58C5	Aketi		Russia	107Q4
Abidjan *Côte d'Ivoire*	144B2	Dem Rep of Congo	146F4	Alessandria *Italy*	76B2
Aboyne *Scot*	61F3	Akita *Japan*	115P7	Ålesund *Nor*	92B3
Abrantes *Port*	72A2	Akmola *Kazakhstan*	109J4	Aleutian Is. *USA*	22J
Abu Zabī *UAE*	133D3	Aksu *China*	126G1	Alexander Arch. *USA*	23J
Abuja *Nig*	145D2	Akron *USA*	18E1	Alexander I. *Ant*	P170
Acapulco *Mexico*	23D4	Akureyrí *Iceland*	92B1	Alexandria *Egypt*	142F1
Accra *Ghana*	145C4	Alabama State *USA*	20E2	Alexandroúpolis *Greece*	81F2
Achill I. *Ireland*	64A3	Alagoas State *Brazil*	37F3	Algeciras *Spain*	73A2
Acklins I. *The Bahamas*	26E2	Alagoinhas *Brazil*	37F4	Alger *Alg*	141D3
Acre State *Brazil*	35B3	Alajuela *Costa Rica*	25C5	Alicante *Spain*	75B2
Adan *Rep Yemen*	132C4	Åland Is. *Fin*	95E3	Alice Springs *Aust*	154C3
Adana *Turk*	130B2	Alaska Pen. *USA*	12C4	Allhābād *India*	127G3
Ad Dakhla *Mor*	140B4	Alaska State *USA*	22J	Al Hudaydah	
Ad Dammām *S Arabia*	131D3	Albacete *Spain*	75B2	Rep Yemen	132C4
Ad Dawhah *Qatar*	131D3	Albany *Aust*	155A4	Al Hufūf *S Arabia*	131C3
Adelaide *Aust*	155C4	Albany *USA*	19F1	Al Jawf *S Arabia*	130B3
Admiralty Is. *Pacific O*	125G4	Al Basrah *Iraq*	131C2	Al Khābūrah *Oman*	133D3
Agadez *Niger*	141D5	Al Baydā' *Libya*	142F1	Al Kuwayt *Kuwait*	131C3
		Alberta State *Canada*	13G4	Al Lādhiqiyah *Syria*	130B2
		Ålborg *Den*	94C4	Al Madīnah *S Arabia*	130B3

Almada *Port*	73A2	
Almaty *Kazakhstan*	109J5	
Al Manāmah *Bahrain*	131D3	
Al Mawsil *Iraq*	130C2	
Al Mukallā *Rep Yemen*	133C4	
Almeria *Spain*	75B2	
Alnwick *Eng*	54F2	
Alorl. *Indon*	124E4	
Alotau *PNG*	125H5	
Alta *Nor*	93E2	
Altay *Mongolia*	111D2	
Amami Ō-shima I. *Japan*	115G4	
Amapá State *Brazil*	36D2	
Amarillo *USA*	17C2	
Amazonas State *Brazil*	35C3	
Ambon *Indon*	124E4	
Amfilokhía *Greece*	80E3	
Amiens *France*	68C2	
Amirante Is. *Indian O*	150F1	
Amman *Jordan*	130B2	
Amorgós I. *Greece*	81F3	
Ampia *Samoa*	165	
Amposta *Spain*	74C1	
Amritsar *India*	126F2	
Amsterdam *Neth*	84A2	
An Najaf *Iraq*	130C2	
Anáfi I. *Greece*	81F3	
Anápolis *Brazil*	37E4	
Anchorage *USA*	12D3	
Ancona *Italy*	77C2	
Andalucia Region *Spain*	73A2	
Andaman Islands *India*	129H4	
Andizhan *Uzbekistan*	109J5	
Andorra la Vella *Andorra*	74C1	
Andorra, Principality *SW Europe*	74C1	
Andros I. *The Bahamas*	24D2	
Ándros *Greece*	81E3	
Angarsk *Rus*	106M4	
Angers *France*	68B2	
Anglesey I. *Wales*	53C4	
Angoulême *France*	69C2	
Anguilla I. *Caribbean Sea*	26G3	
Anhui Province *China*	114F3	
Anjou Province *France*	68B2	
Ankara *Turk*	130B2	
'Annaba *Alg*	141D3	
Annapolis *USA*	18F2	
Annecy *France*	71D2	
Annobón I. *Eq Guinea*	145D3	
Anqing *China*	114F3	
Anshan *China*	112G2	
Anshun *China*	117E4	
Antalya *Turk*	130B2	
Antananarivo *Madag*	151E2	
Antarctic Circle *Ant*	P170	
Antequera *Spain*	73B2	
Anticosti I. *Canada*	15M5	
Antigua I. *Caribbean Sea*	26G3	
Antipodes Is. *NZ*	165	
Antofagasta *Chile*	40B5	
Antrim *N Ire*	65E2	
Antsirabe *Madag*	151E2	
Antsiranana *Madag*	150E2	
Antwerpen *Belg*	70C1	
Anyang *China*	112F3	
Aomori *Japan*	113J2	
Aosta *Italy*	76B1	
Aparri *Phil*	120E2	
Apatity *Rus*	93G2	
Apeldoorn *Neth*	84B2	
Appleby-in-Westmorland *Eng*	53E3	
Aqaba *Jordan*	130B3	
Ar Riyāḍ *S Arabia*	130C3	
Aracaju *Brazil*	37F4	
Aracena *Spain*	73A2	
Arad *Rom*	88E3	
Aran I. *Ireland*	64C1	
Aran Is. *Ireland*	66B3	
Aranda de Duero *Spain*	72B1	
Arbatax *Sardegna*	78B3	
Arbroath *Scot*	63F4	
Arcachon *France*	69B3	
Arch de los Chonos *Chile*	41B7	
Archangel *Rus*	102F3	
Ardabīl *Iran*	131C2	
Ardara *Ireland*	64C2	
Arendal *Nor*	94B4	
Arequipa *Peru*	35B4	
Arezzo *Italy*	77C2	
Argenton-S-Creuse *France*	69C2	
Argos *Greece*	80E3	
Århus *Den*	94C4	
Arica *Chile*	35B4	
Arisaig *Scot*	62C4	
Arizona State *USA*	16B2	
Arkansas State *USA*	18D2	
Arklow *Ireland*	67E3	
Arles *France*	71C3	
Armagh *N Ire*	65E2	
Arnhem *Neth*	84B2	
Arrochar *Scot*	62D4	
Arran I. *Scot*	62C5	
Arta *Greece*	80E3	
Artois Province *France*	68C1	
Arua *Uganda*	146G4	
Aruba I. *Caribbean Sea*	27F4	
Arusha *Tanz*	147G5	
Arvida *Canada*	15L5	
Arvika *Sweden*	94C4	
Asahikawa *Japan*	113J2	
Asansol *India*	129G3	
Āseb *Eth*	147H3	
Ashford *Eng*	56H6	
Ashikaga *Japan*	115N8	
Ashington *Eng*	54F2	
Ashkhabad *Turkmenistan*	108G6	
Asmera *Eritrea*	143G3	
Astipálaia I. *Greece*	81F3	
Astrakhan' *Rus*	108F5	
Asturias Region *Spain*	72A1	
Asunción *Par*	38E5	
Aswân *Egypt*	142G2	
Asyût *Egypt*	142G2	
At. Maturin *Eg*	
At. Ta'il *S Arabia*	132C3	
Isles of Scilly	59A8	
Atar *Maur*	140B4	
Atbara *Sudan*	142G3	
Athenry *Ireland*	66C3	
Athens *Greece*	81E3	
Athínai *Greece*	81E3	
Athlone *Ireland*	66D3	
Atlanta *USA*	18E2	
Atyrau *Kazakhstan*	108G5	
Auckland *NZ*	157G4	
Auckland Is. *NZ*	165	
Augsburg *FRG*	91C3	
Augusta *Aust*	155A4	
Augusta Georgia *USA*	18E2	
Augusta Maine *USA*	19G1	
Augustow *Pol*	86E2	
Aulie-Ata *Kazakhstan*	109J5	
Austin *USA*	23D2	
Auvergne Province *France*	71C2	
Auxerre *France*	70C2	
Aveiro *Port*	72A1	
Avellino *Italy*	79C2	
Avesta *Sweden*	94D3	
Avezzano *Italy*	77C2	
Aviemore *Scot*	61E3	
Avignon *France*	71C3	
Avila *Spain*	74B1	
Avilés *Spain*	72B1	
Axel Heiberg I. *Canada*	14J2	
Axminster *Eng*	59E7	
Áyios Evstrátios I. *Greece*	81F3	
Aylesbury *Eng*	56G6	
Ayr *Scot*	62D5	
Az Zawiyah *Libya*	141E3	

B

Babar I. *Indon*	124E4	
Babuyan I. *Phil*	120E2	
Bacau *Rom*	89F3	
Bacolod *Phil*	120E2	
Badajoz *Spain*	73A2	
Badalona *Spain*	74C1	
Bafatá *Guinea-Bissau*	144A1	
Baffin Island *Canada*	14K2	
Bagé *Brazil*	38E6	
Baghdad *Iraq*	130C2	
Baghlán *Afghan*	126E2	
Baguio *Phil*	120E2	
Bahamas Is.,The, *Caribbean Sea*	26E1	
Bahawalpur *Pak*	126F3	
Bahía Blanca *Arg*	40C6	
Bahia State *Brazil*	37E4	
Baia Mare *Rom*	88E3	
Baicheng *China*	112K2	
Baker I. *Pacific O*	165	
Bakhtaran *Iran*	131C2	
Baku *Azerbaijan*	108F5	
Bala *Wales*	53D5	
Balbriggan *Ireland*	67E3	
Balearic Is. *Spain*	74C2	
Bali I. *Indon*	123D4	
Balikpapan *Indon*	123D4	
Balkhash *Kazakhstan*	109J5	
Ballachulish *Scot*	62C4	
Ballantrae *Scot*	62D5	
Ballarat *Aust*	157D4	
Ballina *Ireland*	64B2	
Ballinasloe *Ireland*	66C3	
Ballygawley *N Ire*	65D2	
Ballymena *N Ire*	65E2	
Baltimore *USA*	19F2	
Bamako *Mali*	144B1	
Bambari *CAR*	146F4	
Bamberg *FRG*	91C3	
Banbury *Eng*	56F5	
Banda Aceh *Indon*	122B3	
Bandar 'Abbās *Iran*	131D3	
Bandar Seri Begawan *Brunei*	123D3	
Bandon *Ireland*	66C5	
Bandundu *Dem Rep of Congo*	146E5	

Bandung *Indon*	123C4	
Banff *Scot*	61F3	
Bangalore *India*	128F4	
Bangassou *CAR*	146F4	
Banghāzi *Libya*	142F1	
Bangka I. *Indon*	123C4	
Bangkok *Thai*	118C2	
Bangor *N Ire*	65F2	
Bangor *Wales*	53C4	
Bangui *CAR*	146E4	
Banja Luka *Bos Herz*	77D2	
Banjarmasin *Indon*	123D4	
Banjul *The Gambia*	140B5	
Bank Is. *Vanuatu*	156F2	
Banks I. *Canada*	12F2	
Bantry *Ireland*	66B5	
Banyuwangi *Indon*	123D4	
Baoding *China*	112F3	
Baoji *China*	117E3	
Baotou *China*	111E2	
Baracaldo *Spain*	72B1	
Barbados I.		
Caribbean Sea	27H4	
Barbuda I. *Leeward Is*	26G3	
Barcelona *Spain*	74C1	
Barcelona *Ven*	34C1	
Bareilly *India*	126F3	
Bari *Italy*	79D2	
Barletta *Italy*	79D2	
Barnaul *Russia*	109K4	
Barnstable *Eng*	58C6	
Barquisimeto *Ven*	34C1	
Barra I. *Scot*	60A3	
Barranquilla *Colombia*	34B1	
Barrow *USA*	12C2	
Barrow-in-Furness *Eng*	53D3	
Barry *Wales*	58D6	
Basel *Switz*	70D2	
Basilan I. *Phil*	120E3	
Basildon *Eng*	56H6	
Basingstoke *Eng*	56F6	
Bassein *Myanmar*	118B2	
Bastia *Corse*	76B2	
Bata *Eq Guinea*	145D2	
Batan I. *Phil*	120E1	
Batang *China*	117D3	
Batangas *Phil*	120E2	
Bath *Eng*	58E6	
Bathurst I. *Aust*	154B2	
Bathurst I. *Canada*	12H2	
Batley *Eng*	55F4	
Battambang *Camb*	118C2	
Batumi *Georgia*	108F5	
Bayeaux *France*	68B2	
Bayonne *France*	69B3	
Bayreuth *FRG*	91C3	
Baza *Spain*	73B2	
Beaufort West *S Africa*	149C4	
Beauly *Scot*	60D3	
Beauvais *France*	68C2	
Béchar *Alg*	141C3	
Bedford *Eng*	56G5	
Beijing *China*	112F3	
Beijing Province *China*	112F3	
Beira *Mozam*	151D2	
Beja *Port*	73A2	
Béjar *Spain*	72A1	
Belcher Is. *Canada*	15K4	
Belcoo *N Ire*	64D2	
Belém *Brazil*	36E2	
Belfast *N Ire*	65F2	
Belfort *France*	70D2	
Belgrade *Yugos*	82E2	
Belhai *China*	117E4	
Belitung *Indon*	123C4	
Belize *Belize*	24B3	
Belle Ile *France*	68B2	
Bello *Colombia*	34B2	
Belmullet *Ireland*	64A2	
Belo Horizonte *Brazil*	37E4	
Belogorsk *Rus*	107O4	
Belopan *Guatemala*	24B3	
Benavente *Spain*	72A1	
Benbecula I. *Scot*	60A3	
Bendigo *Aust*	157D4	
Benevento *Italy*	79C2	
Bengbu *China*	114F3	
Benguela *Angola*	148B2	
Benicarló *Spain*	74C1	
Benidorm *Spain*	75B2	
Benin City *Nig*	145D2	
Benxi *China*	112G2	
Berat *Alb*	80D2	
Berbera *Somalia*	147H3	
Bergamo *Italy*	76B1	
Bergen *Nor*	94B3	
Berkner I. *Ant*	P170	
Berlin *FRG*	85C2	
Bermuda I. *Atlantic O*	19G2	
Bern *Switz*	70D2	
Berry Province *France*	68C2	
Berwick-upon-Tweed		
Eng	54F2	
Besançon *France*	70D2	
Betanzos *Spain*	72A1	
Beverley *Eng*	55G4	
Beyla *Guinea*	144B2	
Beyrouth *Leb*	130B2	
Béziers *France*	71C3	
Bhagalpur *India*	127G3	
Bhamo *Myanmar*	118B1	
Bhopal *India*	128F3	
Biak I. *Indon*	125F4	
Bialystok *Pol*	86E2	
Bideford *Eng*	58C6	
Biel *Switz*	70D2	
Bikaner *India*	126F3	
Bilaspur *India*	129G3	
Billings *USA*	16D1	
Bilbao *Spain*	72B1	
Bioko I. *Atlantic O*	145D2	
Bir Moghrein *Maur*	140B4	
Birkenhead *Eng*	53D4	
Birmingham *Eng*	56F5	
Birmingham *USA*	18E2	
Birobidzhan *Russia*	107P5	
Birr *Ireland*	66D3	
Bishkek *Kyrgyztan*	109J5	
Bishop Auckland *Eng*	54F3	
Biskra *Alg*	141D3	
Bismarck *USA*	17C1	
Bismarck Arch.		
Pacific O	125H4	
Bissau *Guinea-Bissau*	144A1	
Bitola *Yugos*	80E2	
Bizerte *Tunisia*	141D3	
Blace *Cro*	82D2	
Blackburn *Eng*	53E4	
Blackpool *Eng*	53D4	
Blagaevgrad *Bulg*	82E2	
Blagoveshchensk		
Russia	107O4	
Blair Atholl *Scot*	62E4	
Blantyre *Malawi*	150D2	
Blida *Alg*	141D3	
Bloemfontein *S Africa*	149C3	
Blönduós *Iceland*	92A1	
Bluefields *Nic*	25C4	
Blyth *Eng*	54F2	
Bo *Sierra Leone*	144A2	
Boa Vista *Brazil*	34C2	
Bobo Dioulasso		
Burkina Faso	144B1	
Bocas del Toro *Panama*	25C5	
Boden *Sweden*	93E2	
Bodmin *Eng*	59C7	
Bodö *Nor*	92C2	
Bodrum *Turkey*	81F3	
Bognor Regis *Eng*	57G7	
Bogor *Indon*	123C4	
Bogotá *Colombia*	34B2	
Bohol *Phil*	120E3	
Boise *USA*	16B1	
Boké *Guinea*	144A1	
Bollnäs *Sweden*	94D3	
Bologna *Italy*	77C2	
Bolton *Eng*	53E4	
Boma *Dem Rep of Congo*	145E3	
Bombay (Mumbai) *India*	124E4	
Bonaire *Caribbean Sea*	27F4	
Bonn *FRG*	90B2	
Boothia Pen. *Canada*	14J2	
Borås *Sweden*	94C4	
Bordeaux *France*	69B3	
Borneo *Indon/Malay*	123D3	
Bornholm I. *Den*	94C4	
Borzya *Russia*	106N4	
Bosanski Brod *Cro*	82D1	
Boston *Eng*	55G5	
Boston *USA*	19F1	
Bouaké *Côte d'Ivoire*	144B2	
Bouar *CAR*	145E2	
Bouârfa *Mor*	141C3	
Boulogne *France*	68C1	
Bounty Is. *NZ*	165	
Bourg-en-Bresse		
France	71D2	
Bourges *France*	68C2	
Bourgogne Province		
France	70C2	
Bournemouth *Eng*	57F7	
Boyle *Ireland*	64C3	
Brač I. *Yugos*	77D2	
Bradford *Eng*	55F4	
Braga *Port*	72A1	
Braila *Rom*	89F3	
Brasília *Brazil*	37E4	
Brasov *Rom*	89F3	
Bratislava *Slovakia*	88D3	
Bratsk *Russia*	106M4	
Braunschweig *FRG*	85C2	
Bray *Ireland*	67E3	
Brazzaville *Congo*	145E3	
Breda *Neth*	84A2	
Bremen *FRG*	84B2	
Bremerhaven *FRG*	84B2	
Brescia *Italy*	76C1	
Bressay *Scot*	61J7	
Bressuire *France*	68B2	
Brest *Belarus*	102D4	
Brest *France*	68B2	
Bretagne Province		
France	68B2	

Briançon *France* 71D3
Briare *France* 70C2
Bridgetown *Barbados* 27H4
Bridgwater *Eng* 58D6
Bridlington *Eng* 55G3
Brighton *Eng* 57G7
Brindisi *Italy* 79D2
Brisbane *Aust* 156E3
Bristol *Eng* 58E6
British Columbia State *Canada* 13F4
Brive-la-Gaillarde *France* 69C2
Brno *Czech* 91D3
Broken Hill *Aust* 155E4
Broome *Aust* 154B2
Brora *Scot* 61E2
Brownsville *USA* 23D3
Bruck an der Mur *Aust* 91D3
Brunei, Sultanate *SE Asia* 123D3
Brussels *Belg* 70C1
Bruxelles *Belg* 70C1
Bryansk *Russia* 102E4
Bucaramanga *Colombia* 34B2
Buchanan *Lib* 144A2
Bucharest *Rom* 83F2
Buckie *Scot* 61F3
Buckingham *Eng* 56F6
Budapest *Hung* 88D3
Bude *Eng* 59C7
Buenaventura *Colombia* 34B2
Buenos Aires *Arg* 40D6
Buenos Aires State *Arg* 38D6
Buffalo *USA* 17C1
Buffalo *USA* 18F1
Builth Wells *Wales* 58D5
Bujumbura *Burundi* 146E5
Bukavu *Dem Rep of Congo* 146F5
Bukhara *Uzbekistan* 108H6
Bukittinggi *Indon* 122C4
Bulawayo *Zim* 149C3
Bumba *Dem Rep of Congo* 146F4
Bunbury *Aust* 155A4
Bundaberg *Aust* 156E3
Bundoran *Ireland* 64C2
Buraydah *S Arabia* 130C3
Burco *Somalia* 147H4
Burgas *Bulg* 83F2
Burgos *Spain* 72B1
Burley *USA* 17B1
Bursa *Turk* 130A1
Buru I. *Indon* 124E4
Bury St. Edmunds *Eng* 56H5
Buta *Dem Rep of Congo* 146F4
Bute *Scot* 62C5
Butte *USA* 17B1
Butuan *Phil* 120E3
Butung I. *Indon* 124E4
Buzau *Rom* 89F3
Byala *Bulg* 83F2
Bydgoszcz *Pol* 86D2
Bylot I. *Canada* 14L2
Bytom *Pol* 88D2

C

Cabanatuan *Phil* 120E2
Cabimas *Ven* 34B1
Cabinda *Angola* 145E3
Cacak *Yúgos* 82E2
Cáceres *Spain* 73A2

Cádiz *Spain* 73A2
Caen *France* 68B2
Caernarfon *Wales* 53C4
Cagayan de Oro *Phil* 120E3
Cagliari *Sardegna* 78B3
Caher *Ireland* 66D4
Cahors *France* 69C3
Caicos Is. *Caribbean Sea* 26E2
Cairns *Aust* 156D2
Cairo *Egypt* 142G1
Calahorra *Spain* 74B1
Calais *France* 68C1
Calama *Chile* 40B5
Calamian Group *Phil* 120D2
Calatayud *Spain* 74B1
Calcutta *India* 129G3
Calgary *Canada* 13G4
Cali *Colombia* 34B2
California State *USA* 16A2
Callao *Peru* 35B4
Calvi *Corse* 76B2
Camagüey *Cuba* 24D2
Cambeltown *Scot* 62C5
Cambridge *Eng* 56H5
Camden *USA* 19F2
Campbell I. *NZ* 165
Campinas *Brazil* 38F5
Campo Grande *Brazil* 37D5
Campos *Brazil* 38F5
Can Tho *Viet* 119C2
Canberra *Aust* 157D4
Cangazjou *China* 112F3
Cannes *France* 71D3
Canterbury *Eng* 56J6
Cap-Haïtien *Haiti* 26E3
Cape Breton I. *Canada* 15M5
Cape Town *S Africa* 149B4
Capri I. *Italy* 79C2
Caracal *Rom* 83E2
Caracaraí *Brazil* 34C2
Caracas *Ven* 34C1
Caransebes *Rom* 88E3
Carbonia *Sardegna* 78B3
Carcassonne *France* 69C3
Cardiff *Wales* 58D6
Cardigan *Wales* 58C5
Carlisle *Eng* 52E3
Carlow *Ireland* 67E4
Carmarthen *Wales* 58C6
Carnarvon *Aust* 154A3
Carolina *Brazil* 37E3
Caroline I. *Kiribati* 162
Caroline Is. *Pacific O* 125G3
Carrick on Shannon *Ireland* 64C3
Carrickmacross *Ireland* 65E3
Carson City *USA* 16B2
Cartagena *Colombia* 34B1
Cartagena *Spain* 75B2
Cartago *Costa Rica* 25C5
Caserta *Italy* 79C2
Cashel *Ireland* 67D4
Casper *USA* 17C1
Cassino *Italy* 79C2
Castellón de la Plana *Spain* 74B2
Castilla La Mancha Region *Spain* 73B2
Castilla y León Region *Spain* 72A1
Castlebar *Ireland* 64B3
Castleford *Eng* 55F4

Castries *St. Lucia* 27G4
Castrovillari *Italy* 79D3
Cat Island *The Bahamas* 26D1
Cataluña Region *Spain* 74C1
Catamarca State *Arg* 40C5
Catania *Italy* 79D3
Catanzaro *Italy* 79D3
Cateraggio *Corse* 76B2
Cavan *Ireland* 65D3
Cayenne *French Guiana* 36D2
Cayman Islands *Caribbean Sea* 24C3
Ceará State *Brazil* 37F3
Cebu I. *Phil* 120E2
Cebu *Phil* 120E2
Cecina *Italy* 76C2
Cefalù *Italy* 79C3
Cerignola *Italy* 79D2
České Budejovice *Czech Rep* 91C3
Ceuta *Spain* 73A2
Ch'ongjin *N Korea* 113G2
Chaco State *Arg* 40C5
Chalon-sur-Saône *France* 71D2
Châlons-sur-Marne *France* 70C2
Chambéry *France* 71D2
Champagne Province *France* 70C2
Chañaral *Chile* 40B5
Chandigarh *India* 126F2
Chang-hua *Taiwan* 120E1
Changchun *China* 112G2
Changde *China* 114F4
Changsha *China* 114F4
Changzhi *China* 112F3
Channel Is. *UK* 59E8
Channel Port-aux-Basques *Canada* 15N5
Chardzhou *Turkmenistan* 108H6
Charleroi *Belg* 70C1
Charleston *USA* 18F2
Charleville *Aust* 156D3
Charlotte *USA* 18E2
Charlottetown *Canada* 15M5
Chartres *France* 68C2
Châteauroux *France* 69C2
Chatham Is. *NZ* 165
Chattanooga *USA* 18E2
Chaumont *France* 70D2
Chaves *Port* 72A1
Cheboksary *Russia* 106M4
Cheju-do I. *S Korea* 114G3
Chelmsford *Eng* 56H6
Cheltenham *Eng* 59E6
Chelyabinsk *Russia* 109H4
Chemnitz *FRG* 91C2
Chen Xian *China* 114F4
Chengdu *China* 117E3
Chennai (Madras) *India* 129G4
Cherbourg *France* 68B2
Cheremkhovo *Russia* 106M4
Cherepovets *Russia* 102E4
Chernigov *Ukraine* 102E4
Chernovtsy *Ukraine* 102D5
Chesham *Eng* 56G6
Chester *Eng* 53E4
Chesterfield Inlet *Canada* 14J3
Chetumal *Mexico* 24B3
Cheyenne *USA* 17C1
Chiang Mai *Thai* 118B2

Place	Ref	Place	Ref	Place	Ref
Chiba Japan	115P9	Compiègne France	70C2	Daloa Côte d'Ivoire	144B2
Chicago USA	18E1	Conakry Guinea	144A2	Da Nang Viet	119C2
Chichester Eng	57G7	Concepción Chile	40B6	Dandong China	112G2
Chiclayo Peru	35B3	Concepción Par	38E5	Dar'ã Syria	130B2
Chifeng China	112F2	Concord USA	19F1	Dar el Beïda Mor	140C3
Chihuahua Mexico	23C3	Concordia Arg	38E6	Dar es Salaam Tanz	147G5
Chi-lung Taiwan	120E1	Connecticut State USA	19F1	Darlington Eng	55F3
Chimbote Peru	35B3	Consett Eng	54F3	Darmstadt FRG	90B3
Chimkent Kazakhstan	109H5	Constanta Rom	83F2	Daroca Spain	74B1
Chingola Zambia	148C2	Constantine Alg	141D3	Daru PNG	125G4
Chippenham Eng	56E6	Contonou Benin	145D2	Darwin Aust	154C2
Chisinau Moldova	108D5	Cook Is. Pacific O	162	Datong China	112F2
Chita Russia	106N4	Cooktown Aust	156D2	Daugavpils Latvia	102D4
Chittagong Bang	129H3	Copenhagen Den	94C4	Dauphine Province France	71D3
Chojnice Pol	85D2	Corby Eng	56G5	Davao Phil	120E3
Chongqing China	117E4	Corcubión Spain	72A1	David Panama	25C5
Chorley Eng	53E4	Córdoba Arg	40C6	Dawson Creek Canada	13F4
Choybalsan Mongolia	112F2	Córdoba Spain	73B2	Dax France	69B3
Christchurch NZ	157G5	Cordoba State Arg	40C6	Dayton USA	18E2
Christmas I. Indian O	123C5	Corfu I. Greece	80D3	Daytona Beach USA	19F4
Chubut State Arg	41C7	Corigliano Italy	79D3	D'Entrecasteaux I. PNG	125H4
Chumphon Thai	118B2	Corinto Nic	25B4	De Aar S Africa	149C4
Church Stretton Eng	58E5	Cork Ireland	66C5	Debre Mark'os Eth	147G3
Churchill Canada	15J4	Coro Ven	34C1	Debrecen Hung	88E3
Cienfuegos Cuba	24C2	Corpus Christi USA	23D3	Dehra Dun India	126F2
Cieza Spain	75B2	Corrientes Arg	40D5	Delaware State USA	19F2
Cimpina Rom	89F3	Corrientes State Arg	38E5	Delhi India	126F3
Cincinnati USA	18E2	Corse I. France	76B2	Den Helder Neth	84A2
Cirebon Indon	123C4	Corumbá Brazil	37D4	Denbigh Wales	53D4
Citta di Castello Italy	77C2	Cosenza Italy	79D3	Denizli Turk	130A2
Ciudad Bolivar Ven	34C2	Cospic Cro	77D2	Denver USA	17C2
Ciudad Guayana Ven	34C2	Cotabato Phil	120E3	Derby Eng	55F5
Ciudad Juárez Mexico	23C2	Cottbus FRG	85C2	Des Moines USA	18D1
Ciudad Real Spain	73B2	Coventry Eng	56F5	Desé Eth	147G3
Ciudad Rodrigo Spain	72A1	Cowes Isle of Wight	57F7	Dessau FRG	85C2
Civitanova Marche Italy	77C2	Craiova Rom	82E2	Detroit USA	18E1
Civitavecchia Italy	77C2	Crawley Eng	56G6	Deva Rom	88E3
Clacton-on-Sea Eng	56J6	Cres I. Cro	77C2	Devon I. Canada	14K2
Clare I. Ireland	64A3	Crete I. Greece	81E3	Dezfûl Iran	131C2
Claremorris Ireland	66B3	Crewe Eng	53E4	Dezhou China	112F3
Clermont Ferrand France	71C2	Crianlarich Scot	62D4	Dhâka Bang	127H3
Cleveland USA	18E1	Crieff Scot	62E4	Idhra Greece	81E3
Clifden Ireland	66A3	Cromer Eng	55J5	Dibrugarh India	127H3
Cloghan Ireland	66D3	Crotone Italy	79D3	Didcot Eng	56F6
Cloncurry Aust	154D2	Cruzeiro do Sul Brazil	35B3	Dieppe France	68C2
Clonmel Ireland	67D4	Cucuí Brazil	34C2	Dijon France	70C2
Cluj-Napoca Rom	88E3	Cúcuta Colombia	34B2	Dili Indon	124E4
Coatbridge Scot	63D5	Cuddalore India	129F4	Dimashq Syria	130B2
Cobán Guatemala	25A3	Cuenca Ecuador	35B3	Dimitrovgrad Bulg	83F2
Cobh Ireland	66C5	Cuenca Spain	74B1	Dingle Ireland	66A4
Cochabamba Bolivia	35C4	Cuiabá Brazil	37D4	Dingwall Scot	60D3
Cochin India	128F5	Culiacán Mexico	23C3	Diré Dawa Eth	147H4
Cocos I. Indian O	122B5	Cumbernauld Scot	63D5	Dist. Fed. State Brazil	37E4
Codó Brazil	37E3	Cumnock Scot	62D5	Disko I. Greenland	14N3
Coimbatore India	128F4	Cupar Scot	63E4	Diyarbakir Turk	130B2
Coimbra Port	72A1	Curaçao Caribbean Sea	27F4	Djelfa Alg	141D3
Colchester Eng	56H6	Curitiba Brazil	38F5	Djibouti Djibouti	147H3
Coleraine N Ire	65E1	Cuttack India	129G3	Dnepropetrovsk Ukraine	108E5
Coll I. Scot	62B4	Cuxhaven FRG	84B2	Dobreta-Turnu-Severin Rom	82E2
Collooney Ireland	64C2	Cuzco Peru	35B4	Dodoma Tanz	147G5
Colmar France	70D2	Cwmbran Wales	58D6	Dôle France	70D2
Colombo Sri Lanka	129F5	Cyprus Med.Sea	130B2	Dolgellau Wales	58D5
Colombus USA	18E2	Czestochowa Pol	88D2	Dombås Nor	92B3
Colón Panama	25D5			Dominica I. Caribbean Sea	27G3
Colonsay I. Scot	62B4	**D**		Domodossola Italy	76B1
Colorado Springs USA	17C2			Doncaster Eng	55F4
Colorado State USA	17C2	Dagupan Phil	120E2	Donegal Ireland	64C2
Columbia USA	18E2	Dakar Sen	140B5	Donetsk Russia	108E5
Columbus USA	20E2	Da Lat Viet	119C2	Dorchester Eng	59E7
Como Italy	76B1	Dali China	117E4	Dornie Scot	60C3
Comodoro Rivadavia Arg	41C7	Dallas USA	23D2		
Comoros Is. Indian O	150E2	Dalmally Scot	62D4		

Place	Ref
Dortmund *FRG*	84B2
Douala *Cameroon*	145D2
Douglas *Isle of Man*	53C3
Dourados *Brazil*	38E5
Dover *Eng*	56J6
Dover *USA*	19F2
Dráma *Greece*	81E2
Drammen *Nor*	94C4
Dresden *FRG*	91C2
Drogheda *Ireland*	67E3
Dubayy *UAE*	133D3
Dublin *Ireland*	67E3
Dubrovnik *Cro*	82D2
Ducie I. *Pacific O*	162
Dudley *Eng*	58E5
Dugi I. *Cro*	77C2
Duisburg *FRG*	84B2
Dukou *China*	117E4
Duluth *USA*	18D1
Dumbarton *Scot*	62D5
Dumfries *Scot*	63E5
Dun Laoghaire *Ireland*	67E3
Dunbar *Scot*	63F5
Dundalk *Ireland*	65E2
Dundee *Scot*	63F4
Dundrum *N Ire*	65F2
Dunedin *NZ*	157G5
Dunfermline *Scot*	63E4
Dungarvan *Ireland*	67D4
Dungiven *N Ire*	65E2
Dunkeld *Scot*	62E4
Dunkerque *France*	68C1
Dunleer *Ireland*	65E3
Durban *S Africa*	151D3
Durham *Eng*	54F3
Durham *USA*	18F2
Durness *Scot*	60D2
Durrës *Alb*	80D2
Durrow *Ireland*	67D4
Dushanbe *Tajikistan*	109H6
Dusseldorf *FRG*	84B2
Duyun *China*	117E4

E

Place	Ref
Eastbourne *Eng*	57H7
East Falkland I. *South Atlantic O*	39D8
East Kilbride *Scot*	63D5
East London *S Africa*	149C4
Eboli *Italy*	79D2
Ecija *Spain*	73A2
Eday I. *Scot*	61F1
Edgeworthstown *Ireland*	67D3
Edinburgh *Scot*	63E5
Edmonton *Canada*	13G4
Efate I. *Vanuatu*	156F2
Egadi I. *Italy*	78C3
Egersund *Nor*	94B4
Eigg I. *Scot*	62B4
Eindhoven *Neth*	84B2
Eisenach *FRG*	91C2
Elba I. *Italy*	76C2
Elblag *Pol*	86D2
Elche *Spain*	75B2
El Djouf *Maur*	140C4
El Dorado *Ven*	34C2
Eldoret *Kenya*	147G4
Eleuthera I. *The Bahamas*	24D1
El Faiyûm *Egypt*	142G2
El Fasher *Sudan*	146F3
El Ferrol *Spain*	72A1
Elgin *Scot*	61E3
El Gîza *Egypt*	142G1
El Golea *Alg*	141D3
El Iskandarîya *Egypt*	142F1
El Khartum *Sudan*	142G3
Ellesmere I. *Canada*	14K2
Ellesmere Port *Eng*	53E4
Ellon *Scot*	61F3
El Minya *Egypt*	142G2
El Obeid *Sudan*	146G3
El Paso *USA*	23C2
El Qâhira *Egypt*	142G1
Elvas *Port*	73A2
Ely *Eng*	56H5
Enarración *Par*	38E5
Ende *Indon*	124E4
Enggano I. *Indon*	122C4
Enna *Italy*	79C3
Ennis *Ireland*	66B4
Enniscorthy *Ireland*	67E4
Enniskillen *N Ire*	65D2
Ennistymon *Ireland*	66B4
Enschede *Neth*	84B2
Entebbe *Uganda*	146G4
Enugu *Nig*	145D2
Epi I. *Vanuatu*	156F2
Erenhot *China*	112F2
Erfurt *FRG*	91C2
Eriskay I. *Scot*	60A3
Erlangen *FRG*	91C3
Erromanga I. *Vanuatu*	156F2
Erzurum *Turk*	130C2
Esbjerg *Den*	94B4
Esfahân *Iran*	131D2
Eskisehir *Turk*	130B2
Esperance *Aust*	155B4
Espírito Santo *Brazil*	37E4
Espíritu Santo I. *Vanuatu*	156F2
Espoo *Fin*	95E3
Essaouira *Mor*	140C3
Essen *FRG*	84B2
Estremoz *Port*	73A2
Evansville *USA*	18E2
Evvoia I. *Greece*	81E3
Exeter *Eng*	59D7
Extremadura Region *Spain*	73A2

F

Place	Ref
Faeroes I. *Den*	92A2
Fair I. *Scot*	61J8
Fairbanks *USA*	12D3
Faisalâbâd *Pak*	126F4
Fakfak *Indon*	124F4
Falcarragh *Ireland*	64C1
Falkirk *Scot*	63E4
Falkland Islands *South Atlantic O*	39D8
Falmouth *Eng*	59B7
Falster I. *Den*	94C5
Falun *Sweden*	94D3
Fano *Italy*	77C2
Farâh *Afghan*	131E2
Fareham *Eng*	57F7
Fargo *USA*	17D1
Faro *Port*	73A2
Faroe I. *Den*	92A2
Farquhar Is. *Indian O*	150F1
Fauske *Nor*	92D2
Faya-Largeau *Chad*	142E3
Fdérik *Maur*	140B4
Felixstowe *Eng*	56J6
Fergana *Uzbekistan*	109J5
Ferkessédougou *Côte d'Ivoire*	144B2
Fermoy *Ireland*	66C4
Ferrara *Italy*	77C2
Fés *Mor*	140C3
Fetlar I. *Scot*	61K7
Feyzâbâd *Afghan*	126F2
Flanarantsoa *Madag*	151E3
Figueras *Spain*	74C1
Fiji Is. *Pacific O*	165
Filiasi *Rom*	82E2
Firenze *Italy*	77C2
Fishguard *Wales*	58C6
Fitzroy Crossing *Aust*	154B2
Fleetwood *Eng*	53D4
Flensburg *FRG*	84B2
Flint I. *Kiribati*	162
Flores I. *Indon*	124E4
Flores *Guatemala*	24B3
Florianópolis *Brazil*	38F5
Florida State *USA*	20E3
Focsani *Rom*	89F3
Foggia *Italy*	79D2
Foligno *Italy*	77C2
Follonica *Italy*	76C2
Forfar *Scot*	63F4
Forlì *Italy*	77C2
Formentera *Spain*	75C2
Formia *Italy*	79C2
Formosa State *Arg*	40C5
Fortaleza *Brazil*	37F3
Fort Augustus *Scot*	60D3
Fort-de-France *Martinique*	27G4
Fort Lauderdale *USA*	21E3
Fort Simpson *Canada*	12F3
Fort William *Scot*	62C4
Fort Yukon *USA*	12D3
Fort Worth *USA*	23D2
Foshan *China*	114F4
Foula I. *Scot*	61H7
Fougères *France*	68B2
Foz do Iguacu *Brazil*	38E5
Fraga *Spain*	74C1
Franca *Brazil*	37E5
Franceville *Gabon*	145E3
Franche-Comte Province *France*	71D2
Francistown *Botswana*	149C3
Frankfort *USA*	18E2
Frankfurt *FRG*	90B2
Fraser I. *Aust*	156E3
Fraserburgh *Scot*	61F3
Frederikshåb *Greenland*	14O3
Frederikshavn *Den*	94C4
Frederikstad *Nor*	94C4
Freetown *Sierra Leone*	144A2
Freiburg *FRG*	90B3
Fremantle *Aust*	155A4
Fresno *USA*	16B2
Frosinone *Italy*	77C2
Ft. Wayne *USA*	18E1
Fuerteventura I. *Canary Is*	140B4
Fujian Province *China*	114F4
Fukui *Japan*	115M8
Fukuoka *Japan*	115H3
Fukushima *Japan*	115P8
Funchal *Madeira*	140B3
Furneaux Group I. *Aust*	157D5

Fürth *FRG*	91C3
Furukawa *Japan*	115P7
Fushun *China*	112G2
Fuxin *China*	112G2
Fuzhou *China*	114F4
Fyn I. *Den*	94C4

G

Gabès *Tunisia*	141D3
Gaborone *Botswana*	149C3
Gainsborough *Eng*	55G4
Gairloch *Scot*	60C3
Galashiels *Scot*	63F5
Galati *Rom*	89F3
Galicia Region *Spain*	72A1
Galle *Sri Lanka*	129G5
Gallipoli *Italy*	79D2
Gällivare *Sweden*	93E2
Galveston *USA*	20D3
Galway *Ireland*	66B3
Gambier Is. *Pacific O*	162
Gamboma *Congo*	145E3
Gandia *Spain*	75B2
Ganzhou *China*	114F4
Gao *Mali*	141C3
Garve *Scot*	60D3
Gascogne Province *France*	69B3
Gateshead *Eng*	54F3
Gauhati *India*	127H3
Gävle *Sweden*	94D3
Gaziantep *Turk*	130B2
Gdansk *Pol*	86D2
Gdynia *Pol*	86D2
Gedaref *Sudan*	147G3
Geelong *Aust*	157D4
Gejiu *China*	117E4
Gela *Italy*	79C3
Gelati *Rom*	89F3
General Santos *Phil*	120E3
Genève *Switz*	71D2
Genova *Italy*	76B2
Gent *Belg*	70C1
George Town *Malay*	122C3
Georgetown *Guyana*	34D2
Georgetown *St. Vincent*	27G4
Georgia State *USA*	20E2
Gera *FRG*	91C2
Geraldton *Aust*	155A3
Gerona *Spain*	74C1
Getafe *Spain*	72B1
Gevgelija *Yugos*	80E2
Ghadámis *Libya*	141D3
Ghât *Libya*	141E4
Gibraltar Colony *SW Europe*	73A2
Gifu *Japan*	115M9
Giglio I. *Italy*	76C2
Gijón *Spain*	72A1
Gilbert Is. *Kiribati*	165
Gilgit *Pak*	126F2
Girvan *Scot*	62D5
Gisborne *NZ*	157G4
Giurgiu *Rom*	83F2
Glasgow *Scot*	63D5
Glenrothes *Scot*	63E4
Gliwice *Pol*	88D2
Gloucester *Eng*	58E6
Gniezno *Pol*	85D2
Gobabis *Namibia*	149B3
Godthåb *Greenland*	14N3
Goiânia *Brazil*	37E4

Goiás State *Brazil*	37E4
Gol *Nor*	94B3
Golmund *China*	111D3
Gomel' *Belarus*	102E4
Gomera *Canary Is*	140B4
Gonaïves *Haiti*	26E3
Gonder *Eth*	147G3
Goole *Eng*	55G4
Gort *Ireland*	66C3
Gorzów Wielkopolski *Pol*	85D2
Göteborg *Sweden*	94C4
Gotland I. *Sweden*	95D4
Göttingen *FRG*	84B2
Goulburn *Aust*	157D4
Gran Canaria *Canary Is*	140B4
Granada *Nic*	25B4
Granada *Spain*	73B2
Grand Bahama I. *The Bahamas*	24D1
Grand Rapids *USA*	18E1
Grandola *Port*	73A2
Graz *Aust*	91D3
Great Abaco I. *The Bahamas*	24D1
Great Exuma I. *The Bahamas*	24D2
Great Inagua I. *The Bahamas*	26E2
Great Nicobar I. *India*	129H5
Great Yarmouth *Eng*	56J5
Greater Antilles Is. *Car*	24D3
Greenland Dependency *N Atlantic O*	1402
Greenock *Scot*	62D5
Greensboro *USA*	18F2
Grenada *Caribbean Sea*	27G4
Grenada, I. *Caribbean Sea*	27G4
Grenadines Is., The *Caribbean Sea*	27G4
Grenoble *France*	71D2
Gretna *Scot*	63E5
Grimsby *Eng*	55G4
Grong *Nor*	92C3
Groningen *Neth*	84B2
Groote Eylandt I. *Aust*	154C2
Grootfontein *Namibia*	149B2
Grosseto *Italy*	77C2
Groznyy *Russia*	108F5
Grudziadz *Pol*	86D2
Guadalajara *Mexico*	23C3
Guadalajara *Spain*	72B1
Guadalcanal I. *Solomon Is*	156E2
Guadalupe I. *Mexico*	22B3
Guadeloupe I. *Caribbean Sea*	26G3
Guam *Pacific O*	121G2
Guangdong Province *China*	114F4
Guangxi Province *China*	117E4
Guangzhou *China*	114F4
Guantánamo *Cuba*	26D2
Guarda *Port*	72A1
Guatemala *Guatemala*	25A4
Guayaquil *Ecuador*	35B3
Guernsey I. *UK*	59E8
Guildford *Eng*	56G6
Guilin *China*	114F4
Guiria *Ven*	34C1

Guiyang *China*	117E4
Guizhou Province *China*	117E4
Gulu *Uganda*	146G4
Guyenne Province *France*	69B3
Gwalior *India*	126F3
Gweru *Zim*	149C2
Gyor *Hung*	88D3

H

Hā'il *S Arabia*	130C3
Haarlem *Neth*	84A2
Hachinohe *Japan*	115P6
Hagen *FRG*	84B2
Haifa *Israel*	130B2
Haikou *China*	114F4
Hailar *China*	112F2
Hainan Dao I. *China*	114F5
Haiphong *Viet*	119C1
Hakodate *Japan*	113J2
Halab *Syria*	130B2
Halden *Nor*	94C4
Halifax *Canada*	15M5
Halifax *Eng*	55F4
Halle *FRG*	85C2
Halmahera I. *Indon*	124E3
Halmstad *Sweden*	94C4
Hamadān *Iran*	131C2
Hamamatsu *Japan*	115M9
Hamar *Nor*	94C3
Hamburg *FRG*	85C2
Hamhung *N Korea*	112G2
Hami *China*	111D2
Hamilton *Canada*	15K5
Hamilton *NZ*	157G4
Hamm *FRG*	84B2
Hammerfest *Nor*	93E1
Hanamaki *Japan*	115P7
Handan *China*	112F3
Hangzhou *China*	114G3
Hannover *FRG*	84B2
Hanoi *Viet*	119C1
Hanzhong *China*	117E3
Haora *India*	129G3
Harare *Zim*	150D2
Harbin *China*	112G2
Härer *Eth*	147H4
Hargeysa *Somalia*	147H4
Harlow *Eng*	56H6
Harris I. *Scot*	60B3
Harrisburg *USA*	18F1
Harrogate *Eng*	55F4
Hartford *USA*	19F1
Hartlepool *Eng*	54F3
Harwich *Eng*	56J6
Hässleholm *Sweden*	94C4
Hastings *Eng*	57H7
Hastings *NZ*	157G4
Haugesund *Nor*	94B4
Havana (La Habana) *Cuba*	24C2
Havant *Eng*	57G7
Hawaii Hawaiian Is.	22H
Hawaiian Is. *Pacific O*	22H
Hawick *Scot*	63F5
Hay River *Canada*	13G3
Heanor *Eng*	55F4
Heard Is. *Indian O*	164
Hebei *China*	112F3
Hefei *China*	114F3
Hegang *China*	112H2
Heidelberg *FRG*	90B3

Heilongjiang Province China	112G2
Helena USA	17B1
Hella Iceland	92A2
Hellín Spain	75B2
Helmsdale Scot	61E2
Helsinborg Sweden	94C4
Helsingfors Fin	95F3
Helsinki Fin	95F3
Henan Province China	114F3
Hengyang China	114F4
Henzada Myanmar	118B2
Herāt Afghan	131E2
Hereford Eng	58E5
Hexham Eng	52E3
Hierro Canary Is	140B4
Hiiumaa I. Estonia	95E4
Himeji Japan	115L9
Hims Syria	130B2
Hinckley Eng	56F5
Hinnøy I. Nor	92D2
Hiroshima Japan	113H3
Hîrsova Rom	83F2
Hispaniola I. Caribbean Sea	26E3
Hitachi Japan	115P8
Ho Chi Minh City Viet	119C2
Hobart Tasmania	157D5
Höfn Iceland	92B2
Hohhot China	112F2
Hokitika NZ	157G5
Hokkaidō I. Japan	113J2
Holguín Cuba	24D2
Holy I. Eng	54F2
Holyhead Wales	53C4
Honiara Solomon Is	156E1
Honolulu Hawaiian Is	22H
Horsham Eng	56G6
Hotan China	110C3
Hotan China	126F2
Hoting Sweden	92D3
Houghton-le-Spring Eng	54F3
Houston USA	20D3
Hovd Mongolia	111D2
Hoy I. Scot	61E2
Hradec-Králové Czech	91D2
Huainan China	114F3
Huambo Angola	148B2
Huancayo Peru	35B4
Huangshi China	114F3
Hubei Province China	114F3
Hubli India	128F4
Huddersfield Eng	55F4
Hudiksvall Sweden	94D3
Hue Viet	119C2
Huelva Spain	73A2
Hughenden Aust	156D3
Humaitá Brazil	35C3
Hunan Province China	114F4
Hunstanton Eng	55H5
Huntly Scot	61F3
Huntsville USA	18E2
Húsavík Iceland	92B1
Hvar I. Cro	77D2
Hwange Zim	148C2
Hyderābād India	128F4
Hyderābād Pak	126E3
Hythe Eng	56J6I

I

Ibadan Nig	145D2

Ibiza Spain	75C2
Ibiza I. Spain	75C2
Ica Peru	35B4
Iceland Republic N Atlantic O	14R3
Idaho State USA	16B1
Igarka Russia	103K3
Igoumenítsa Greece	80E3
Ikaría I. Greece	81F3
Ile d'Oléron France	69B2
Ile de Noirmoutier France	68B2
Ile de Ré France	69B2
Ilebo Dem Rep of Congo	146F5
Iles d'Hyéres France	71D3
Ilfracombe Eng	58C6
Iliodhrómia I. Greece	81E3
Illinois State USA	18E1
Iloilo Phil	120E2
Ilorin Nig	145D2
Imperatriz Brazil	37E3
Impfondo Congo	146E4
Imphāl India	127H3
In Salah Alg	141D4
Indiana State USA	18E1
Indianapolis USA	18E2
Indore India	128F3
Inhambane Mozam	151D3
Inner Hebrides Scot	62B4
Inner Mongolia Province China	112F2
Innsbruck Aust	91C3
Inuvik Canada	12E3
Invararay Scot	62C4
Invercargill NZ	157F5
Inverness Scot	61D3
Inverurie Scot	61F3
Ioannina Greece	80E3
Íos I. Greece	81F3
Iowa State USA	18D1
Ipoh Malay	122C3
Iquique Chile	35B5
Iquitos Peru	35B3
Iráklion Greece	81F3
Iringa Tanz	150D1
Irkutsk Russia	106M4
Irvine Scot	62D5
Isafördhur Iceland	92A1
Ischia I. Italy	79C2
Ise Japan	115M9
Ishinomaki Japan	115P7
Isiro Dem Rep of Congo	146F4
Isla Blanquilla I. Ven	27G4
Isla Coiba Panama	25C5
Isla de Chilloé I. Chile	41B7
Isla de la Bahía Hondur	24B3
Isla de la Juventud Cuba	24C2
Isla del Rey Panama	25D5
Isla Los Rogues I. Ven	27F4
Isla Margarita I. Ven	27G4
Isla Santa Inés I. Chile	41B7
Islâmabād Pak	126F2
Island of Newfoundland Canada	15N4
Islas Canarias Spain	140B4
Islay I. Scot	62B5
Isle of Man UK	53C3
Isle of Wight Eng	57F7
Isles of Scilly Eng	59A8

Istanbul Turk	130A1
Isthmus of Kra Thai	118B3
Itabuna Brazil	37F4
Itaituba Brazil	37D3
Iturup I. Russia	113J2
Ivalo Fin	93F2
Ivangrad Yugos	82D2
Ivanovo Russia	102F4
Iwaki Japan	115P8
Iwo Jima Japan	121G1
Izhevsk Russia	109G4
Izmir Turk	130A2

J

Jabalpur India	128F3
Jackson USA	20D2
Jacksonville USA	20E2
Jacmel Haiti	26E3
Jaén Spain	73B2
Jaffna Sri Lanka	129G5
Jaipur India	126F3
Jajce Bos Herz	77D2
Jakarta Indon	123C4
Jalgaon India	128F3
Jamaica Caribbean Sea	122C4
Jambi Indon	126F2
Jammu India	126F2
Jamnager India	128E3
Jämsänkoski Fin	95F3
Jamshedpur India	129G3
Jardines de la Reina Cuba	24D2
Jarvis I. Pacific O	162
Jawa I. Indon	123C4
Jayapura Indon	125G4
Jedburgh Scot	63F5
Jefferson City USA	18D2
Jelenia Góra Pol	91D2
Jena FRG	91C2
Jequié Brazil	37E4
Jerez de la Frontera Spain	73A2
Jersey I. UK	59E8
Jerusalem Israel	130B2
Jhansi India	126F3
Ji'an China	114F4
Jiamusi China	112H2
Jiangsu Province China	114F3
Jiangxi Province China	114F4
Jiddah S Arabia	132B3
Jihlava Czech	91D3
Jilin China	112G2
Jilin Province China	113G2
Jima Eth	147G4
Jinan China	112F3
Jingdezhen China	114F4
Jinhua China	114F4
Jining China	114F3
Jinzhou China	112G2
Jiujiang China	114F4
João Pessoa Brazil	37F3
Jodhpur India	126F3
Johannesburg S Africa	149C3
John O'Groats Scot	61E2
Johnson I. Pacific O	159
Johor Baharu Malay	122C3
Jokkmokk Sweden	93D2
Jóló I. Phil	120E3
Jönköping Sweden	94C4
Jörn Sweden	93E2
Jos Nig	145D2

Jotunheimen *Nor*	94B3
Juázeiro *Brazil*	37E3
Juba *Sudan*	146G4
Jujuy State *Arg*	40C5
Julianehåb *Greenland*	14O3
Juneau *USA*	12E4
Jura I. *Scot*	62C5
Jylland I. *Den*	94B4
Jyväskylä *Fin*	93F3

K

Kábul *Afghan*	126E2
Kaduna *Nig*	145D1
Kaédi *Maur*	140B5
Kaesŏng *N Korea*	112G3
Kagoshima *Japan*	115H3
Kaifeng *China*	114F3
Kailua *Hawaiian Is*	22H
Kairouan *Tunisia*	141D3
Kajaani *Fin*	93F3
Kåkinåda *India*	129G4
Kalabáka *Greece*	80E3
Kalajoki *Fin*	93E3
Kalámai *Greece*	80E3
Kalaupapa *Hawaiian Is*	22H
Kalémié	
Dem Rep of Congo	146F5
Kalgoorlie *Aust*	155B4
Kálimnos I. *Greece*	81F3
Kaliningrad *Russia*	102D4
Kalisz *Pol*	86D2
Kalmar *Sweden*	94D4
Kamaishi *Japan*	115P7
Kamina	
Dem Rep of Congo	148C1
Kampala *Uganda*	146G4
Kananga	
Dem Rep of Congo	146F5
Kanazawa *Japan*	115M8
Kandahár *Afghan*	126E2
Kandalaksha *Russia*	102E3
Kandangan *Indon*	123D4
Kandy *Sri Lanka*	129G5
Kaneohe *Hawaiian Is*	22H
Kangaroo I. *Aust*	155C4
Kankan *Guinea*	144B1
Kano *Nig*	145D1
Kānpur *India*	126G3
Kansas City *USA*	18D2
Kansas State *USA*	17D2
Kao-hsiung *Taiwan*	120E1
Kaolack *Sen*	144A1
Karáchi *Pak*	128E3
Karaganda *Kazakhstan*	109J5
Karbalá *Iraq*	130B2
Karcag *Hung*	88B3
Karlobag *Cro*	77D2
Karlovac *Cro*	77D1
Karlshamn *Sweden*	94C4
Karlskoga *Sweden*	94C4
Karlskrona *Sweden*	94D4
Karlsruhe *FRG*	90B3
Karlstad *Sweden*	94C4
Kárpathos I. *Greece*	81F3
Karshi *Uzbekistan*	109H6
Kasama *Zim*	150D2
Kasese *Uganda*	146G4
Kashi *China*	110B3
Kásos I. *Greece*	81F3
Kassala *Sudan*	143G3
Kassel *FRG*	90B2

Kastoria *Greece*	80E2
Kateríni *Greece*	80E2
Katherine *Aust*	154C2
Kathmandu *Nepal*	127G3
Katowice *Pol*	88D2
Katsina *Nig*	145D1
Kauai I. *Hawaiian Is*	22H
Kaunas *Lithuania*	95E5
Kaválla *Greece*	81E2
Kawaihae *Hawaiian Is*	22H
Kawasaki *Japan*	115N9
Kayes *Mali*	144A1
Kayseri *Turk*	130B2
Kazan *Russia*	108F4
Kazanlŭk *Bulg*	83F2
Kazan-rettő *Japan*	121G1
Kéa *Greece*	81E3
Kecskemét *Hung*	88D3
Kediri *Indon*	123D4
Keetmanshoop *Namibia*	149B3
Kefallinía I. *Greece*	80E3
Keflavík *Iceland*	92A2
Keighley *Eng*	55F4
Keith *Scot*	61F3
Kelang *Malay*	122C3
Kells *Ireland*	67E3
Kemerovo *Russia*	109K4
Kemi *Fin*	93E2
Kemijarvi *Fin*	93F2
Kendal *Eng*	53E3
Kendari *Indon*	124E4
Kengtung *Myanmar*	118B1
Kenitra *Mor*	140C3
Kenmare *Ireland*	66B5
Kenora *Canada*	15J5
Kentucky State *USA*	18E2
Kep. Anambas I. *Indon*	123C3
Kep. Aru I. *Indon*	124F4
Kep. Banggai *Indon*	124E4
Kep. Kai I. *Indon*	124F4
Kep. Leti I. *Indon*	124E4
Kep. Mentawai, Arch.	
Indon	122B4
Kepno *Pol*	88D2
Kep. Sangihe I. *Indon*	124E3
Kep. Sula *Indon*	124E4
Kep. Talaud I. *Indon*	124E3
Kep. Tanimbar I. *Indon*	124F4
Kep. Togian *Indon*	124E4
Kerch *Russia*	108E5
Kerguelen Is. *Indian O*	164
Kérkira *Greece*	80D3
Kermadec Is. *Pacific O*	165
Kermán *Iran*	131D2
Keswick *Eng*	52E3
Key West *USA*	20E3
Khabarovsk *Russia*	107P5
Khálkis *Greece*	81E3
Khaniá *Greece*	81E3
Kharagpur *India*	129G3
Khar'kov *Russia*	108E4
Khartoum *North Sudan*	142G3
Khartoum *Sudan*	142G3
Khíos I. *Greece*	81F3
Khulna *Bang*	129G3
Kiel *FRG*	85C2
Kielce *Pol*	88E2
Kigali *Rwanda*	146G5
Kigoma *Tanz*	146F5
Kikladhes Is. *Greece*	81E3
Kikwit	
Dem Rep of Congo	146E5

Kildare *Ireland*	67E3
Kilkenny *Ireland*	67D4
Killarney *Ireland*	66B4
Kilmarnock *Scot*	62D5
Kilrush *Ireland*	66B4
Kimberley *S Africa*	149C3
Kindia *Guinea*	144A1
Kindu	
Dem Rep of Congo	146F5
King I. *Aust*	157D4
Kings Lynn *Eng*	55H5
Kingston *Jamaica*	24D3
Kingston-upon-Hull *Eng*	55G4
Kingswood *Eng*	58E6
Kingussie *Scot*	61D3
Kinnegad *Ireland*	67D3
Kintyre *Scot*	62C5
Kinvarra *Ireland*	66C3
Kiribati Is. *Pacific O*	165
Kiritimati *Kiribati*	162
Kirkby Stephen *Eng*	53E3
Kirkcaldy *Scot*	63E4
Kirkenes *Nor*	93G2
Kirkūk *Iraq*	130C2
Kirkwall *Scot*	61F2
Kirov *Russia*	108F4
Kirovabad *Ukraine*	108F5
Kiruna *Sweden*	93E2
Kisangani	
Dem Rep of Congo	146F4
Kiskunfélegyháza	
Hung	88D3
Kismaayo *Somalia*	147H5
Kisumu *Kenya*	147G5
Kita-Kyūshū *Japan*	113H3
Kithira I. *Greece*	81E3
Kíthnos *Greece*	81E3
Kitwe *Zambia*	149C2
Kiyev *Ukraine*	102E4
Kladno *Czech Rep*	91C2
Klagenfurt *Aust*	91C3
Klaipeda *Lithuania*	102D4
Klerksdorp *S Africa*	149C3
Knoxville *USA*	18E2
Kōbe *Japan*	115L9
København *Den*	94C4
Kolding *Den*	94B4
Koblenz *FRG*	90B2
Kochi *Japan*	113H3
Kodiak I. *USA*	22J
Kofu *Japan*	115N9
Kokkola *Fin*	93E3
Kolhāpur *India*	128F4
Köln *FRG*	90B2
Koloma *Russia*	102E4
Kolwezi	
Dem Rep of Congo	148C2
Komatsu *Japan*	115M8
Komotini *Greece*	81F2
Kompong Cham *Camb*	119C2
Kompong Som *Camb*	118C2
Komsomol'sk na-Amure	
Russia	107P4
Konin *Pol*	86D2
Konjic *Bos Herz*	82D2
Konya *Turk*	130B2
Kópavogur *Iceland*	92A2
Korčë *Alb*	80E2
Korcula I. *Cro*	77D2
Kórinthos *Greece*	80E3
Koriyama *Japan*	115P8
Kornat I. *Cro*	77D2

Korsør *Den*	94C4	
Kós I. *Greece*	81F3	
Kosice *Slovakia*	88E3	
Kosovska-Mitrovica *Yugos*	82E2	
Koszalin *Pol*	85D2	
Kota *India*	126F3	
Kota Baharu *Malay*	122C3	
Kota Kinabalu *Malay*	123D3	
Kotka *Fin*	95F3	
Kotlas *Russia*	102F3	
Kotor *Yugos*	82D2	
Kowloon *Hong Kong*	119D1	
Kragujevac *Yugos*	82E2	
Kraków *Pol*	85D2	
Kramsfors *Sweden*	92D3	
Kranj *Slovenia*	77C1	
Krasnodar *Russia*	108E5	
Krasnovodsk *Turkmenistan*	108G5	
Krasnoyarsk *Russia*	106L4	
Krefeld *FRG*	84B2	
Kristiansand *Nor*	94B4	
Kristianstad *Sweden*	94C4	
Krivoy Rog *Ukraine*	108E5	
Krk I. *Cro*	77C1	
Kruscevac *Yugos*	82E2	
Kuala Lumpur *Malay*	122C3	
Kuala Terengganu *Malay*	122C3	
Kuching *Malay*	123D3	
Kulata *Bulg*	82E2	
Kumamoto *Japan*	115H3	
Kumanovo *Macedonia*	82E2	
Kumasi *Ghana*	144B2	
Kumashir I. *Russia*	113J2	
Kunming *China*	117E4	
Kuopio *Fin*	93F3	
Kupang *Indon*	124E5	
Kuril'skye Ostrova *Russia*	107R5	
Kurnool *India*	128F4	
Kursk *Russia*	108E4	
Kushiro *Japan*	113J2	
Kwangju *S Korea*	112G3	
Kyle of Lochalsh *Scot*	60C3	
Kyoto *Japan*	115L9	
Kyzyl *Russia*	106L4	
Kzyl Orda *Kazakhstan*	109H5	

L

Laâyoune *Mor*	140B4	
Labé *Guinea*	144A1	
Lábrea *Brazil*	35C3	
Labytnangi *Russia*	103H3	
La Ceiba *Honduras*	25B4	
La Coruña *Spain*	72A1	
Lae *PNG*	125G4	
La Flèche *France*	68B2	
Lagos *Nig*	145D2	
Lagos *Port*	73A2	
La Habana (Havana) *Cuba*	24C2	
Lahore *Pak*	126F2	
Lahti *Fin*	95F3	
Lai Chau *Viet*	118C1	
Lairg *Scot*	60D2	
Lajes *Brazil*	128F4	
Lakshadweep Is. *India*	128F4	
Lambaréné *Gabon*	145E3	
Lamía *Greece*	80E3	
Lampedusa I. *Italy*	79C3	

Lampione I. *Italy*	78C3	
Lanai I. *Hawaiian Is*	22H	
Lanark *Scot*	63E5	
Lancaster *Eng*	53E3	
Lang Son *Viet*	70D2	
Langres *France*	71C3	
Languedoc Province *France*	71C3	
Lansing *USA*	18E1	
Lanzarote I. *Canary Is*	140B4	
Lanzhou *China*	113E3	
Laoag *Phil*	120E2	
Lao Cai *Viet*	119C1	
La Palma *Canary Is*	140B4	
La Pampa State *Arg*	40C5	
La Paz *Bolivia*	35C4	
La Plata *Arg*	38E6	
Laredo *USA*	23D3	
Largs *Scot*	62D2	
La Rioja Region *Spain*	72B1	
La Rioja State *Arg*	40C5	
Lárisa *Greece*	80E3	
La Rochelle *France*	69B2	
La Roda *Spain*	75B2	
La Romana *Dom Rep*	26F3	
La Serena *Chile*	40B5	
Lashio *Myanmar*	118B1	
Iasi *Rom*	89F3	
Las Palmas de Gran Canaria *Canary Is*	140B4	
La Spezia *Italy*	76B2	
Lastovo I. *Cro*	77D2	
Las Vegas *USA*	16B2	
Latina *Italy*	79C2	
La Tortuga I. *Ven*	27F4	
Launceston *Tasmania*	157D5	
Laurencekirk *Scot*	63F4	
Lausanne *Switz*	71D2	
Laut I. *Indon*	123D4	
Laval *France*	68B2	
L'Aquila *Italy*	77C2	
Leeds *Eng*	55F4	
Leeuwarden *Neth*	84B2	
Leeward Is. *Caribbean Sea*	26G3	
Legazpi *Phil*	120E2	
Leicester *Eng*	55F5	
Leipzig *FRG*	91C2	
Leiria *Port*	72A2	
Le Havre *France*	68C2	
Le Mans *France*	68C2	
Lens *France*	70C1	
León *Mexico*	23C3	
León *Nic*	25B4	
León *Spain*	72A1	
Lérida *Spain*	74C1	
Léros I. *Greece*	81F3	
Lerwick *Scot*	61J7	
Les Caye *Haiti*	26E3	
Leshan *China*	117E4	
Leskovac *Yugos*	82E2	
Lesotho, Kingdom *S Africa*	149C3	
Lesser Antilles Is. *Caribbean Sea*	27F4	
Lésvós I. *Greece*	81F3	
Letterkenny *Ireland*	65D2	
Levkás I. *Greece*	80E3	
Lewes *Eng*	57H7	
Lewis I. *Scot*	60B2	
Leyte I. *Phil*	120E2	

Lhasa *China*	116D4	
Lianoyang *China*	112G2	
Lianyungang *China*	114F3	
Liaoning Province *China*	112G3	
Liaoyuan *China*	112G2	
Liberec *Czech Rep*	91D2	
Libreville *Gabon*	145D2	
Lichinga *Mozam*	150D2	
Liége *Belg*	70D1	
Liepája *Latvia*	95E4	
Likasi *Dem Rep of Congo*	148C2	
Lille *France*	70C1	
Lillehammer *Nor*	94C3	
Lilongwe *Malawi*	150D2	
Lima *Peru*	35B4	
Limerick *Ireland*	66C4	
Límnos *Greece*	81F3	
Limoges *France*	69C2	
Limón *Costa Rica*	25C5	
Limousin Province *France*	69C2	
Linares *Spain*	73B2	
Lincang *China*	117E4	
Lincoln *Eng*	55G4	
Lincoln *USA*	17D1	
Linfen *China*	114F3	
Linköping *Sweden*	94D4	
Linosa I. *Italy*	79C3	
Linz *Aust*	91C3	
Lipari I. *Italy*	79C3	
Lisbon *Port*	73A2	
Lisburn *N Ire*	65E2	
Lisieux *France*	68C2	
Little Rock *USA*	18D2	
Liuzhou *China*	117E4	
Livanátais *Greece*	80E3	
Liverpool *Eng*	53E4	
Livingston *Scot*	63E5	
Livingstone *Zambia*	148C2	
Livno *Bos Herz*	77D2	
Livorno *Italy*	76C2	
Ljubljana *Slovenia*	77C1	
Llandrindod Wells *Wales*	58D5	
Lobito *Angola*	148B2	
Lochboisdale *Scot*	60A3	
Lochgilphead *Scot*	62C4	
Lochinver *Scot*	60C2	
Lochmaddy *Scot*	60A3	
Locri *Italy*	79D3	
Lódz *Pol*	86D2	
Logroño *Spain*	72B1	
Loja *Ecuador*	35B3	
Loja *Spain*	73B2	
Lolland I. *Den*	94C5	
Lom *Bulg*	82E2	
Lombok I. *Indon*	123D4	
Lome *Togo*	145D2	
London *Eng*	56G6	
Londonderry *N Ire*	65D1	
Long Island *The Bahamas*	26E2	
Long Island I. *USA*	19F1	
Longford *Ireland*	67D3	
Lorca *Spain*	75B2	
Lord Howe I. *Aust*	157F4	
Lorient *France*	68B2	
Los Angeles *USA*	16B2	
Los Mochis *Mexico*	23C3	
Losinj I. *Yugos*	63E5	

Louisiana State USA	20D2
Louisville USA	18E2
Loukhi Russia	93G2
Louth Eng	55G4
Loznica Yugos	82D2
Lu'an China	114F3
Luanda Angola	148B1
Luang Prabang Laos	118C2
Lubango Angola	148B2
Lubbock USA	17C2
Lübeck FRG	85C2
Lublin Pol	88E2
Lubumbashi	
Dem Rep of Congo	148C2
Lucca Italy	76C2
Lucknow India	127G3
Lüda China	112G3
Lüderitz Namibia	149B3
Ludhiana India	126F2
Ludvika Sweden	94D3
Luga Russia	95F4
Lugo Spain	72A1
Luleå Sweden	58C5
Lundy I. Eng	58C6
Luohe China	114F3
Luoyang China	114F3
Lurgan N Ire	65E2
Lusaka Zambia	148C2
Luton Eng	56G6
Luxembourg Lux	70D2
Luxor Egypt	142G2
Luzern Switz	70D2
Luzhou China	117E4
Luzon I. Phil	120E2
L'viv Ukraine	102D5
Lybster Scot	61E2
Lycksele Sweden	93D3
Lyon France	71C2

M

Maastricht Neth	90B2
Ma'ān Jordan	130B2
Macapá Brazil	36D2
Macau Port	119D1
Macclesfield Eng	53E4
Maceió Brazil	37F3
Mackay Aust	156D3
Macomer Sardegna	78B2
Mâcon France	71C2
Macon USA	20E2
Macquarie I. NZ	165
Madang PNG	125G4
Madeira I. Atlantic O	140B3
Madison USA	18E1
Madras (Chennai) India	129G4
Madrid Spain	72B1
Madura I. Indon	123D4
Madurai India	128F5
Mafia I. Tanz	150D1
Mafikeng S Africa	149C3
Magadan Russia	105R4
Magdeburg FRG	85C2
Magnitogorsk Russia	109G4
Mahajanga Madag	150E3
Mahalapye Botswana	149C3
Mahón Spain	74C2
Maidstone Eng	56H6
Maiduguri Nig	145E3
Maine Province France	68B2
Maine State USA	19F1
Mainland I.	
Scot Orkney I	61J7

Mainland I.	
Scot Shetland I	61E1
Mainz FRG	90E3
Maitland Aust	157E4
Maizuru Japan	115L9
Majene Indon	123D4
Majorca I. Spain	74C2
Makarska Cro	77D2
Makhachkala Russia	108F5
Makkah S Arabia	132B3
Makó Hung	88B3
Makurdi Nig	145D2
Malabo Bioko I	145D2
Malaga Spain	73B2
Malakal Sudan	146G4
Malang Indon	123D4
Malanje Angola	148B1
Malatya Turk	130B2
Malden I. Kiribati	162
Maldives Is. Indian O	128F5
Malekula I. Vanuatu	156F2
Mallaig Scot	60C3
Mallow Ireland	66C4
Malmö Sweden	94C4
Malton Eng	55G3
Mamou Guinea	144A1
Man Cote d'Ivoire	144B2
Mana Hawaiian Is	22H
Manacor Spain	74C2
Manado Indon	124E3
Managua Nic	25B4
Manakara Madag	151E3
Manaus Brazil	35C3
Manchester Eng	53E4
Mandal Nor	94B4
Mandalay Myanmar	118B1
Manfredonia Italy	77D2
Mangalia Rom	83F2
Mangalore India	128F4
Manila Phil	120E2
Manitoba State Canada	13H4
Manizalés Colombia	34B2
Mannheim FRG	90B3
Manokwari Indon	124F4
Mansfield Eng	55F4
Manta Ecuador	34A3
Mantes France	68C2
Manzanillo Cuba	24D2
Manzhouli China	112F2
Maoming China	114F4
Maputo Mozam	151D3
Maracaibo Ven	34B1
Maradi Nig	145D1
Maranhão State Brazil	37E3
Marbella Spain	73B2
Marburg FRG	90B2
Mardan Pak	126F2
Mar del Plata Arg	38E6
Margate Eng	56J6
Maribor Cro	77D1
Marie-Galante I.	
Caribbean Sea	26G3
Mariestad Sweden	94C4
Marília Brazil	38F5
Marmaris Turkey	81F3
Maroua Cameroon	145E3
Marquesas Is. Pacific O	162
Marrakesh Mor	140C3
Marseille France	71D3
Marshall Is. Pacific O	159
Martinique I.	
Caribbean Sea	27G4

Mary Turkmenistan	108H6
Maryland State USA	19F2
Masaya Nic	25B4
Masbate I. Phil	120E2
Maseru Lesotho	149C3
Mashhad Iran	131D2
Masirah I. Oman	133D3
Masqat Oman	133D3
Massa Italy	76C2
Massachusetts State	
USA	19F1
Matadi	
Dem Rep of Congo	145E3
Matagalpa Nic	25B4
Matamoros Mexico	23D3
Matanzas Cuba	24C2
Mataram Indon	123D4
Matlock Eng	55F4
Mato Grosso Do Sul State	
Brazil	37D4
Mato Grosso State	
Brazil	37D4
Matsue Japan	113H3
Matsumoto Japan	115M6
Matsusaka Japan	115M9
Matsuyama Japan	113H3
Maui Hawaiian Is	22H
Mauritius I. Indian O	151F4
Mayaguana I.	
The Bahamas	26E2
Maybole Scot	62D5
Mayotte I. Indian O	150E2
Mazār-e Sharif Afghan	126E2
Mazatlán Mexico	23C3
Mbabane Swaziland	151D3
Mbandaka	
Dem Rep of Congo	146E4
Mbarara Uganda	146G5
Mbeya Tanz	150D1
Mbuji-Mayi	
Dem Rep of Congo	146F5
Meaux France	70C2
Medan Indon	122B3
Medellín Colombia	34B2
Medgidia Rom	83F2
Medicine Hat Canada	13G4
Meerut India	126F3
Meiktila Myanmar	116B1
Meknès Mor	140C3
Melaka Malay	122C3
Melbourne Aust	157D4
Melilla Spain	73B2
Melitopol' Ukraine	108E5
Melo Urug	38E6
Melun France	70C2
Melvich Scot	61E2
Melville I. Aust	154C2
Melville I. Canada	12G2
Melville Pen. Canada	14D3
Memphis USA	18E2
Mende France	71C3
Mendoza Arg	40C6
Mendoza State Arg	40C6
Menongue Angola	148C2
Menzanares Spain	73B2
Merauke Indon	125G4
Mercedes Arg	40C6
Mergui Arch. Myanmar	118B2
Mérida Mexico	20E3
Mérida Spain	73A2
Merthyr Tydfil Wales	58D6
Mesolóngian Greece	80E3

184

Messina Italy	79D3
Metz France	70D2
Mexicali USA	16B2
México Mexico	23D4
Meymaneh Afghan	126E2
Miami USA	21E3
Mianyany China	117E3
Michigan State USA	18E1
Michurin Bulg	83F2
Midway Is. Pacific O	159
Mikkeli Fin	95F3
Mikonos I. Greece	81F3
Milano Italy	76B1
Mildura Aust	155D4
Milford Haven Wales	58B6
Millau France	71C3
Milos Greece	81E3
Milton Keynes Eng	56G5
Milwaukee USA	18E1
Minas Gerais State Brazil	37E4
Minatinán Mexico	20D4
Mindanao Phil	120E3
Mindoro I. Phil	120E2
Minna Nig	145D2
Minneapolis USA	18D1
Minnesota State USA	17D1
Minorca I. Spain	74C2
Minsk Belarus	102D4
Miranda de Ebro Spain	72B1
Miri Malay	123D3
Mirzapur India	127G3
Misiones State Arg	38E5
Miskolc Hung	88E3
Misool Indon	124F4
Misrâtah Libya	141E3
Mississippi State USA	20D2
Missouri State USA	18D2
Mito Japan	115P8
Mits'iwa Eth	143G3
Miyako Japan	115P7
Miyazaki Japan	115H3
Mizusawa Japan	115P7
Mjölby Sweden	94D4
Mlawa Pol	86E2
Mljet I. Cro	82D2
M. Lampang Thai	118B2
M. Nakhon Sawan Thai	118C2
Mo-i-Rana Nor	92C2
Mobile USA	20E2
Moçambique Mozam	150E2
Modena Italy	77C2
Moffat Scot	63E5
Mogadishu Somalia	147H4
Mogilev Belurus	102E4
Mokp'o S Korea	112G3
Molde Nor	92B3
Mollendo Peru	35B4
Molokai I. Hawaiian Is	22H
Mombasa Kenya	147G5
Monaco Monaco	71D3
Monaghan Ireland	65E2
Mondovi Italy	76B2
Mongu Zambia	148C2
Monopoli Italy	79D2
Monreal del Campo Spain	74B1
Monrovia Lib	144A2
Montana State USA	17B1
Montargis France	70C2
Montauban France	69C3
Montbéliard France	70D2
Monte Cristi Haiti	26E3
Montego Bay Jamaica	24D3
Monteria Colombia	34B2
Monterrey Mexico	23C3
Montes Claros Brazil	37E4
Montevideo Urug	38E6
Montgomery USA	20E2
Montluçon France	71C2
Montpelier USA	19F1
Montréal Canada	15L5
Montrose Scot	63F4
Montserrat I. Caribbean Sea	26G3
Monza Italy	76B1
Mopti Mali	144B1
Mora Sweden	94C3
Moradabad India	126F3
Morioka Japan	115P7
Moroni Comoros	150E2
Morotai I. Indon	124E3
Morwell Aust	157D4
Moshi Tanz	147G5
Mosjöen Nor	92C2
Moskva Russia	105E4
Moss Nor	94C4
Mossoró Brazil	37F3
Mostaganem Alg	141D3
Mostar Bos Herz	82D2
Motherwell Scot	63E5
Motril Spain	73B2
Moulins France	71C2
Moulmein Myanmar	118B2
Moundou Chad	145E4
Mount Gambier Aust	155D4
Mount Isa Aust	154C3
M. Phitsanulok Thai	118C2
Mt. Magnet Aust	155A3
Mtwara Tanz	150E2
Mudanjiang China	112G2
Mufulira Zambia	148C2
Muhos Fin	93F3
Mulhouse France	70D2
Mull I. Scot	62C4
Mullingar Ireland	67D3
Multan Pak	126F2
Mumbai (Bombay) India	124E4
Muna I. Indon	124E4
München FRG	91C3
Mungbere Dem Rep of Congo	146F4
Munster FRG	84B2
Muonio Fin	93E2
Mughisho Somalia	147H4
Murcia Spain	75B2
Murcia Region Spain	75B2
Murmansk Russia	103E3
Musselburgh Scot	63E5
Mutare Zim	151D2
Mwanza Tanz	146F5
Mwene Ditu Dem Rep of Congo	146F5
My Tho Viet	119C2
Myingyan Myanmar	118B1
Myitkyina Myanmar	118B1
Mymensingh Bang	127H3
Mysore India	128F4

N

Naas Ireland	67E3
Naga Phil	120E2
Nagano Japan	115N8
Nagaoka Japan	115N8
Nagasaki Japan	115G3
Nagercoil India	128F5
Nagoya Japan	115M9
Nagpur India	128F3
Nagykanizsa Hung	91D3
Nain Canada	15M4
Nairn Scot	61E3
Nairobi Kenya	147G5
Nakhodka Russia	107P5
Nakhon Ratchasima Thai	118C2
Nakhon Si Thammarat Thai	118B3
Nakuru Kenya	147G5
Nam Dinh Viet	119C1
Namangan Uzbekistan	109J5
Namibe Angola	148B2
Nampula Mozam	150D2
Nanchang China	114F4
Nanchong China	117E3
Nancy France	70D2
Nanjing China	114F3
Nanning China	117E4
Nanping China	114F4
Nantes France	68B2
Nantong China	114G3
Nanyang China	114F3
Napoli Italy	79C2
Narbonne France	71C3
Narva Estonia	95F4
Narvik Nor	92D2
Nar'yan Mar Russia	103G3
Nashville USA	18E2
Nassau The Bahamas	24D1
Natal Brazil	37F3
Natuna Besar I. Indon	123C3
Navarra Region Spain	74B1
Náxos I. Greece	81F3
Ndjamena Chad	145E3
Ndola Zambia	148C2
Neápolos Greece	81E3
Near Islands USA	22J
Nebraska State USA	17C1
Negros Phil	120E3
Nei Mongol Zizhiqu Province China	112F2
Neiva Colombia	34B2
Nellore India	129G4
Nelson Eng	53E4
Nelson NZ	157G5
Nenagh Ireland	66C4
Neubrandenburg FRG	85C2
Neumünster FRG	85B2
Neuquén Arg	40C6
Neuquén State Arg	40C6
Nevada State USA	16B2
Nevers France	70C2
Newark USA	19F1
Newark-on-Trent Eng	55G4
New Britain I. Pacific O	125G4
Newcastle Aust	157E4
Newcastle-upon-Tyne Eng	54F3
New Delhi India	126F3
Newfoundland Canada	15M4
New Georgia Solomon Is	156E1
New Hampshire State USA	19F1
New Jersey State USA	19F1
New Mexico State USA	17C2
New Orleans USA	20E3
Newport Isle of Wight	57F7
Newport Wales	58E6
Newquay Eng	59B7

Place	Ref
New Ross *Ireland*	67E4
Newry *N Ire*	65E2
New South Wales State *Aust*	157D4
Newton Aycliffe *Eng*	54F3
Newton Stewart *Scot*	62D6
Newtown-abbey *N Ire*	65F2
New York *USA*	19F1
New York State *USA*	18F1
Ngaoundére *Cameroon*	145E4
Nguru *Nig*	145E3
Nha Trang *Viet*	119C2
Niamey *Niger*	145D1
Nias I. *Indon*	122B4
Nice *France*	71D3
Nicobar I. *India*	129H5
Nicosia *Cyprus*	130B2
Niigata *Japan*	115N8
Nijmegen *Neth*	84B2
Nikel *Russia*	93G2
Nikolayev *Russia*	108E5
Nîmes *France*	71C3
Ningbo *China*	114G4
Ningxia Province *China*	111E3
Nioro du Sahel *Mali*	140C5
Niort *France*	69B2
Nis *Yugos*	82E2
Nitra *Slovakia*	88D3
Niue I. *Pacific O*	165
Nivernais Province *France*	70C2
Nizamabad *India*	128F4
Nizhny Novgorod *Russia*	108F4
Nizhniy Tagil *Russia*	109H4
Nkongsamba *Cameroon*	145D2
Nong Khai *Thai*	119C2
Norfolk *USA*	19F2
Norfolk I. *Aust*	157F3
Noril'sk *Russia*	103K3
Normandie Province *France*	68B2
Norrköping *Sweden*	94D4
Norseman *Aust*	155B4
North Bay *Canada*	15L5
North Carolina State *USA*	18E2
North Dakota State *USA*	17C1
Northern Mariana I. *Pacific O*	121G2
Northern Ter. State *Aust*	154C2
North I. *NZ*	157G4
North Uist I. *Scot*	60A3
Northwest Territories State *Canada*	12G3
Norwich *Eng*	56J5
Notodden *Nor*	94B4
Nottingham *Eng*	55F5
Nouadhibou *Maur*	140B4
Nouakchott *Maur*	140B5
Nouméa *Nouvelle Calédonie*	156E1
Nouvelle Calédonie I. *Pacific O*	156E1
Novara *Italy*	76B1
Nova Scotia *Canada*	15M5
Novaya Zemlya *Russia*	103G2
Novi Pazar *Yugos*	82E2
Novi Sad *Yugos*	82D1
Novokuznetsk *Russia*	109K4
Novorosslysk *Russia*	108E5
Novosibirsk *Russia*	109K4
Novosibirskiye Ostrova I. *Russia*	104Q2
N. Ronaldsay I. *Scot*	61F1
Nuku'alofa *Tonga*	165
Nukus *Uzbekistan*	108G5
Numazu *Japan*	115N9
Nunivak I. *USA*	12B3
Nürnberg *FRG*	91B3
Nyala *Sudan*	146F3
Nyíregyháza *Hung*	88E3
Nykoping *Sweden*	94D4
Nyngan *Aust*	157D4
Nzérékoré *Guinea*	144B2

O

Place	Ref
Oahu I. *Hawaiian Is*	22H
Oban *Scot*	62C4
Obi I. *Indon*	124E4
Odawara *Japan*	115N9
Odda *Nor*	94B3
Odemira *Port*	83A2
Odense *Den*	94C4
Odessa *Ukraine*	108D5
Odessa *USA*	23C2
Offenbach *FRG*	90B2
Ogaki *Japan*	115M9
Ogasawara-Shotó *Jap*	121G1
Ogbomosho *Nig*	145D2
Ogden *USA*	17B1
Ohrid *Macedonia*	80E2
Okaya *Japan*	115N8
Okayama *Japan*	113H3
Okazaki *Japan*	115M9
Okehampton *Eng*	59C7
Okhotsk *Russia*	105Q4
Okinawa I. *Japan*	113G4
Oklahoma City *USA*	17D2
Oklahoma State *USA*	17D2
Öland I. *Sweden*	94D4
Olbia *Sardegna*	78B2
Oldenburg *FRG*	84B2
Olomouc *Czech Rep*	91D3
Olsztyn *Pol*	86E2
Olympia *USA*	16A1
Omagh *N Ire*	65D2
Omaha *USA*	17D1
Omdurman *Sudan*	142G3
Omsk *Russia*	109J4
Onitsha *Nig*	145D2
Ontario State *Canada*	15J4
Oostende *Belg*	70C1
Opole *Pol*	88D2
Oradea *Rom*	86E3
Oran *Alg*	141C3
Orange *Aust*	157D4
Orange *France*	71C3
Orbetello *Italy*	77C2
Orléanais Province *France*	68C2
Örebro *Sweden*	94D4
Oregon State *USA*	16A1
Orel *Russia*	108E4
Orenburg *Russia*	108G4
Orense *Spain*	72A1
Orkney Is. *Scot*	61E1
Orlando *USA*	20E3
Orléans *France*	68C2
Örnsköldsvik *Sweden*	93D3
Orsk *Russia*	109G4
Oruro *Bolivia*	35C4
Ôsaka *Japan*	155L9
Oshogbo *Nig*	145D2
Osijek *Cro*	82D1
Oskarshamn *Sweden*	94D4
Oslo *Nor*	94C4
Osnabrück *FRG*	84B2
Osorno *Chile*	41B7
Östersund *Sweden*	92C3
Ostia *Italy*	77C2
Ostrava *Czech Rep*	88D3
Ôsumi-shoto *Japan*	113H3
Oswestry *Eng*	53D5
Otaru *Japan*	113J2
Ottawa *Canada*	15L5
Ouagadougou *Burkina Faso*	144C3
Ouahigouya *Burkina Faso*	144B1
Ouargla *Alg*	141D3
Oudtshoorn *S Africa*	149C4
Oujda *Mor*	141C3
Oulu *Fin*	93F2
Outer Hebrides *Scot*	60A3
Oviedo *Spain*	72A1
Oxford *Eng*	56F6
Oyem *Gabon*	145E4

P

Place	Ref
Padang *Indon*	122C4
Paderborn *FRG*	84B2
Pag I. *Cro*	77D2
Pagai Selatan I. *Indon*	123C4
Pagai Utara I. *Indon*	122B4
Pahala *Hawaiian Is*	22H
Pais Vasco Region *Spain*	72B1
Paisley *Scot*	62D5
Palan I. *Pacific O*	158
Palangkaraya *Indon*	123D4
Palau *Caroline Is*	124F3
Palawan I. *Phil*	120D2
Palembang *Indon*	122C4
Palencia *Spain*	72B1
Palermo *Italy*	79C3
Palma de Mallorca *Spain*	74C2
Palmerston North *NZ*	157G5
Palmi *Italy*	79D3
Palmyra *Pacific O*	160
Palu *Indon*	123D4
Pamplona *Spain*	74B1
Panamá *Panamá*	25D5
Panay I. *Phil*	120E2
Pangkalpinang *Indon*	123D4
Pantelleria I. *Italy*	78C3
Papa Westray I. *Scot*	61F1
Pará State *Brazil*	37D3
Paracel I. *S China Sea*	119D2
Paracin *Yugos*	82E2
Paraíba State *Brazil*	37F3
Parakou *Benin*	145D2
Paramaribo *Suriname*	36D2
Paraná *Arg*	40C6
Parana State *Brazil*	38E5
Parepare *Indon*	123D4
Paris *France*	68C2
Parkano *Fin*	95E3
Parma *Italy*	76C2
Parnaíba *Brazil*	37E3
Pärnu *Estonia*	95E4
Pasadena *USA*	16B2
Passo Fundo *Brazil*	38E5

Pasto Colombia	34B2
Patna India	127G3
Pátrai Greece	80E3
Pau France	69B3
Pavlodar Kazakhstan	109J4
P.Dolak I. Indon	125F4
Pec Yugos	82E2
Pécs Hung	88D3
Peebles Scot	63E5
Pegu Myanmar	118B2
Pekanbaru Indon	122C3
Peking (Beijing) China	112F3
Pello Fin	93E2
Pelopónnisos I. Greece	80E3
Pemba Mozam	150E2
Pemba I. Tanz	147G5
Pembroke Wales	58C6
Pennsylvania State USA	18F1
Penrith Eng	52E3
Penza Russia	108F4
Penzance Eng	59B7
Pereira Colombia	34B2
Périgueux France	69C2
Perm Russia	109G4
Pernambuco State Brazil	37F3
Perpignan France	71C3
Perth Aust	155A4
Perth Scot	62E4
Perugia Italy	77C2
Pescara Italy	77C2
Peshawar Pak	126F2
Peterborough Eng	56G5
Peterhead Scot	61G3
Petropavlovsk Kazakhstan	109H4
Petropavlovsk Kamchatskiy Russia	105R4
Petrozavodsk Russia	102E3
Philadelphia USA	19F1
Phnom Penh Camb	119C2
Phoenix USA	16B2
Phoenix Is. Kiribati	165
Phuket I. Thai	118B3
Piacenza Italy	76B1
Piauí State Brazil	37E3
Picardie Province France	70C2
Pierre USA	17C1
Pietermaritzburg S Africa	149D3
Pietersburg S Africa	149C3
Pila Pol	85D2
Pilos Greece	80E3
Pinar del Rio Cuba	24C2
Pingliang China	117E3
Piombino Italy	76C2
Piraiévs Greece	81E3
Pírgos Greece	80E3
Pirot Yugos	82E2
Pisa Italy	76C2
Pitcairn I. Pacific O	162
Piteå Sweden	93E2
Pitesti Rom	83E2
Pitlochry Scot	62E4
Pittsburgh USA	18F1
Piura Peru	35A3
Plasencia Spain	72A1
Pleven Bulg	83E2
Ploiesti Rom	83F2
Plovdiv Bulg	83E2
Plymouth Eng	59C7
Plzen Czech	91C3
Podgorica Yugos	82D2
Pointe-á-Pitre Guadeloup	26G3
Pointe Noire Congo	145E3
Poitiers France	69C2
Poitou Province France	69B2
Polla Italy	79D2
Poltava Ukraine	108E5
Ponce Puerto Rico	26F3
Ponferrada Spain	72A1
Pontevedra Spain	72A1
Pontianak Indon	123C4
Poole Eng	57F7
Pori Fin	95E3
Port Augusta Aust	155C4
Port au Prince Haiti	26E3
Port Elizabeth S Africa	149C4
Port Gentil Gabon	145D3
Port Harcourt Nig	145D2
Port Headland Aust	154A3
Portland USA	16A
Port Laoise Ireland	67D3
Port Louis Mauritius	151F4
Port Moresby PNG	125G4
Pôrto Alegre Brazil	38E5
Port of Spain Trinidad	27G4
Porto Novo Benin	145D2
Porto Port	72A1
Porto Torres Sardegna	78B2
Porto Vecchio Corse	76B2
Pôrto Velho Brazil	35C3
Port Pirie Aust	155C4
Portrush N Ireland	65E1
Port Said Egypt	142G1
Portsmouth Eng	57F7
Port Sudan Sudan	143G3
Port Talbot Wales	58D6
Poso Indon	124E4
Potchefstroom S Africa	149C3
Potenza Italy	79D2
Potosí Bolivia	35C4
Potsdam FRG	85C2
Poznan Pol	85D2
Prato Italy	77C2
Preston Eng	53E4
Preswick Scot	62D5
Pretoria S Africa	149C3
Prince Edward I. Can	15M5
Prince George Canada	13F4
Prince of Wales I. Canada	12H2
Prince Rupert Canada	13F4
Principe I. W Africa	145D2
Pristina Czech	82E2
Prokop'yevsk Russia	109K4
Prome Myanmar	118B2
Provence Province France	71D3
Providence USA	19F1
Prudhoe Bay USA	12D2
Przemys'l Pol	88E3
Pskov Russia	102D4
Pucallpa Peru	35B3
Puebla Mexico	23D4
Puerto Armuelles Panama	25C5
Puerto Ayacucho Ven	34C2
Puerto Barrios Guatemala	25B3
Puerto Cabezas Nic	25C4
Puerto Cortés Honduras	25B4
Puerto Juárez Mexico	20E3
Puerto Montt Chile	41B7
Puerto Plata Dom Rep	26E3
Puerto Rico I. Caribbean Sea	26F3
Puertollano Spain	73B2
Pula Cro	77C2
Pune India	128F4
Punta Arenas Chile	41B8
Puntarenas Costa Rica	25C5
Pusan S Korea	113G3
Puttgarden FRG	85C2
Pyongyang China	112G3

Q

Qamdo China	117D3
Qazvin Iran	131C2
Qena Egypt	142G2
Qingdao China	112G3
Qinghai Province China	111D3
Qingjiang China	114F3
Qinhuangdao China	112F2
Qiqihar China	112G2
Qom Iran	131D2
Qu Xian China	114F4
Quanzhou China	114F4
Québec Canada	15L5
Québec State Canada	15L4
Queen Charlotte Is. Canada	13E4
Queen Elizabeth Is. Canada	12G2
Queensland State Aust	154E03
Quelimane Mozam	150D2
Quetta Pak	126E3
Quezaltenango Guatemala	25A4
Quezon City Phil	120E2
Qui Nhon Viet	119C2
Quilon India	128F5
Quimper France	68B2
Quito Ecuador	34B3

R

Raasay I. Scot	60B3
Rab I. Cro	77C2
Raba Indon	123D4
Rabat Mor	140C3
Radom Pol	88E2
Raipur India	129G3
Rajkot India	128F3
Raleigh USA	18F2
Ramsey Isle of Man	53C3
Rancagua Chile	40B6
Ranchi India	129G3
Randers Den	94C4
Rangpur Bang	127G3
Rapid City USA	17C1
Rasht Iran	131C2
Ráth Luirc Ireland	66C4
Rathlin I. N Ire	65E1
Ratlam India	128F3
Rauma Fin	95E3
Ravenna Italy	77C2
Rawalpindi Pak	126F2
Razgrad Bulg	83F2
Reading Eng	56G6
Recife Brazil	37F3
Redon France	68B2
Regensburg FRG	91B3
Reggane Alg	141D4
Reggio di Calabria Italy	79D3

Reggio nell'Emilia *Italy*	76C2	
Regina *Canada*	13H4	
Reims *France*	70C2	
Renell I. *Solomon Is*	156F2	
Rennes *France*	68B2	
Reno *USA*	16B2	
Resistencia *Arg*	40D5	
Resolution I. *Canada*	14M3	
Réunion I. *Indian O*	151F4	
Reykjavík *Iceland*	92A2	
Rhode Island State *USA*	19F1	
Rhodes I. *Greece*	81F3	
Rhum I. *Scot*	62B4	
Rhyl *Wales*	53E4	
Richmond *USA*	19F2	
Riga *Latvia*	102D4	
Rijeka *Cro*	77C1	
Rimini *Italy*	77C2	
Rîmnicu Vîlcea *Rom*	89E3	
Ringwood *Eng*	57F7	
Rio Branco *Brazil*	35C3	
Rio de Janeiro *Brazil*	38F5	
Rio de Janeiro State		
Brazil	38F5	
Río Gallegos *Arg*	41C8	
Rio Grande *Brazil*	38E5	
Rio Grande do Norte State		
Brazil	37F3	
Rio Grande do Sul State		
Brazil	38E5	
Río Negro State *Arg*	41C7	
Ripon *Eng*	55F3	
Roanne *France*	71C2	
Rochdale *Eng*	53E4	
Rochester *Eng*	56H6	
Rochester *USA*	18D1	
Rockford *USA*	18E1	
Rockhampton *Aust*	156E3	
Rødbyhavn *Den*	94C5	
Ródhos *Greece*	81F3	
Roman *Rom*	89F3	
Rome *Italy*	77C2	
Ronda *Spain*	73A2	
Rondônia State *Brazil*	35C4	
Roscoff *France*	88B2	
Roscommon *Ireland*	66C3	
Roscrea *Ireland*	67D4	
Roseau *Dominica*	27G3	
Rosslare *Ireland*	67E4	
Rostock *FRG*	85C2	
Rostov-na-Donu *Russia*	108E5	
Rotherham *Eng*	55F4	
Roti I. *Indon*	124E5	
Rotterdam *Neth*	84A2	
Rouen *France*	68C2	
Round I. *Mauritius*	151F4	
Rousay I. *Scot*	61E1	
Roussillon Province		
France	69C3	
Rovaniemi *Fin*	93F2	
Royal Tunbridge Wells		
Eng	56H6	
Ruffec *France*	69C2	
Rugby *Eng*	56F5	
Rugen I. *FRG*	85C2	
Ruma *Yugos*	82D1	
Runcorn *Eng*	53E4	
Ruoqiang *China*	110C3	
Ruse *Bulg*	83F2	
Ruteng *Indon*	124E4	
Ryazan' *Russia*	108E4	

Rybinsk *Rus*	102E4	
Rybnik *Pol*	88D2	
Ryūkyū Is. *Japan*	113G4	
Rzeszów *Pol*	88E2	

S

Saarbrucken *FRG*	90B3	
Saaremaa I. *Est*	95E4	
Sabac *Yugos*	82D2	
Sabadell *Spain*	74C1	
Sabhã *Libya*	141E4	
Sacramento *USA*	16A2	
Sadiya *India*	127H3	
Safi *Mor*	140C3	
Sagunto *Spain*	74B2	
Saintes *France*	69B2	
Sakai *Japan*	115L9	
Sakata *Japan*	115N7	
Sakhalin I. *Russia*	107Q4	
Sakishima guntō *Japan*	115G4	
Salãlah *Oman*	133D4	
Salamanca *Spain*	72A1	
Salangen *Nor*	92D2	
Salayar I. *Indon*	124E4	
Salbris *France*	68C2	
Salem *India*	128F4	
Salem *USA*	16A1	
Salerno *Italy*	79C2	
Salford *Eng*	53E4	
Salisbury *Eng*	56F6	
Salo *Fin*	95E3	
Salonta *Rom*	82B1	
Salt Lake City *USA*	17B1	
Salta *Arg*	40C5	
Salta State *Arg*	40C5	
Saltillo *Mexico*	23C3	
Salto *Urug*	38E6	
Salvador *Brazil*	37F4	
Salzburg *Aust*	91C3	
Salzgitter-Bad *FRG*	85C2	
Samar I. *Phil*	120E2	
Samara *Russia*	108G4	
Samarinda *Indon*	123D4	
Samarkand *Uzbekistan*	109H6	
Samoa *Pacific O*	165	
Sámos I. *Greece*	81F3	
Samothráki I. *Greece*	81F2	
Samsun *Turk*	130B1	
San *Mali*	144B1	
San Antonio *USA*	23D3	
San'a *Rep Yemen*	132C4	
San Benedetto del Tronto		
Italy	77C2	
San Cristóbal *Ven*	34B2	
San Cristóbal I.		
Solomon Is	156F2	
Sancti Spíritus *Cuba*	24D2	
Sandakan *Malay*	123D3	
Sanday I. *Scot*	61F1	
San Diego *USA*	16B2	
Sandoy I. *Den*	92A2	
San Fernando *Phil*	120E2	
San Francisco *USA*	16A2	
Sanjō *Japan*	115N8	
San José *Costa Rica*	25C5	
San Jose *USA*	16A2	
San Juan *Arg*	40C6	
San Juan *Puerto Rico*	26F3	
San Juan del Norte *Nic*	25C4	
San Juan del Sur *Nic*	25B4	
San Juan State *Arg*	40C6	
San Julián *Arg*	41C7	

San Luis Potosí *Mexico*	23C3	
San Luis State *Arg*	40C6	
Sanmenxia *China*	114F3	
San Marino *San Marino*	77D2	
San Miguel de Tucuman		
Arg	40C5	
San Miguel *El Sal*	25B4	
San Pedro Sula		
Honduras	25B3	
San Remo *Italy*	76B2	
San Salvador *El Sal*	25B4	
San Salvador I.		
The Bahamas	26E1	
San Sebastián *Spain*	74B1	
Santa Ana *El Sal*	25B4	
Santa Catarina State		
Brazil	38E5	
Santa Clara *Cuba*	24C2	
Santa Cruz *Bolivia*	35C4	
Santa Cruz Is. *S*		
olomon Is	156F24	
Santa Cruz State *Arg*	41B7	
Santa Fé *Arg*	40C6	
Santa Fe *USA*	17C2	
Santa Isabel I.		
Solomon Is	156E1	
Santa Marta *Colombia*	34B1	
Santander *Spain*	72B1	
Santarém *Brazil*	37D3	
Santarém *Port*	73A2	
Santa Rosa *Arg*	40C6	
Santa State *Arg*	40C5	
Santiago *Chile*	40B6	
Santiago *Dom Rep*	26E3	
Santiago *Panama*	25C5	
Santiago de Compostela		
Spain	72A1	
Santiago de Cuba *Cuba*	24D3	
Santiago del Estero		
Arg	40C5	
Santo Domingo		
Dom Rep	26F3	
São Carlos *Brazil*	38F5	
São Luís *Brazil*	37E3	
São Paulo *Brazil*	38F5	
São Paulo State *Brazil*	38F5	
São Tomé I. *W Africa*	145D2	
São Tomé and Príncipe Rep.		
W Africa	145D2	
Sapporo *Japan*	113J2	
Sapri *Italy*	79D2	
Sarajevo *Bos Herz*	82D2	
Saratov *Russia*	108F4	
Sardegna *Italy*	78B2	
Sark I. *UK*	59E8	
Sarrion *Spain*	74B1	
Sasebo *Japan*	115G3	
Saskatchewan State		
Canada	13H4	
Saskatoon *Canada*	13H4	
Sassari *Sardegna*	78B2	
Sassandra *Côte d'Ivoire*	144B2	
Sassnitz *FRG*	85C2	
Satu Mare *Rom*	88E3	
Sault Ste Marie *Canada*	15K5	
Savannah *USA*	20E2	
Savannakhet *Laos*	119C2	
Savoie Province *France*	71D2	
Savona *Italy*	76B2	
Savonlinna *Fin*	93F3	
Saxmundham *Eng*	56J5	

Saynshand *Mongolia*	112F2	Sibolga *Indon*	122B3	South Georgia I.	
Scarborough *Eng*	55G3	Sibu *Malay*	123D3	South Atlantic O	39G8
Schwerin *FRG*	85C2	Sichuan Province *China*	117E3	South Island *NZ*	157F5
Scourie *Scot*	60C2	Sicila *Italy*	79C3	Southport *Eng*	53D4
Scunthorpe *Eng*	55G4	Sidi Bel Abbés *Alg*	141C3	South Ronaldsay *Scot*	61F2
Seattle *USA*	16A1	Siedlce *Pol*	86E2	South Shields *Eng*	54F3
Seaward Pen. *USA*	12B3	Siegen *FRG*	90B2	South Uist I. *Scot*	60A3
Sebes *Rom*	88E3	Siena *Italy*	77C2	Sovetskaya Gavan'	
Ségou *Mali*	144B1	Sifnos *Greece*	81E3	*Russia*	107Q5
Segovia *Spain*	72B1	Sigüenza *Spain*	72B1	Soweto *S Africa*	149C3
Seinajoki *Fin*	93E3	Siguirí *Guinea*	144B1	Spalding *Eng*	55G5
Sekondi *Ghana*	145C4	Sikasso *Mali*	144B1	Split *Cro*	77D2
Selby *Eng*	55F4	Sikinos *Greece*	81F3	Spokane *USA*	16B1
Semarang *Indon*	123D4	Simeulue I. *Indon*	122B4	Spratly Islands	
Semipalatinsk		Singkawang *Indon*	123C3	*S China Sea*	119D2
Kazakhstan	109K4	Sintra *Port*	73A2	Springfield *USA*	18D2
Sendai *Japan*	115P7	Sioux Falls *USA*	17D1	Springfield *USA*	18E2
Senlis *France*	70C2	Siping *China*	112G2	Springs *S Africa*	149C3
Senmen *Eng*	59B7	Sipora I. *Indon*	122B4	Srinagar *India*	126F2
Sens *France*	70C2	Siracusa *Italy*	79D3	S Ronaldsay *Scot*	61F2
Seoul *S Korea*	112G3	Síros *Greece*	81E3	S Severo *Italy*	77D2
Seram I. *Indon*	124E4	Sisak *Cro*	77D1	Sta. Cruz de Tenerife	
Sergino *Russia*	109H3	Sittwe *Myanmar*	118B1	*Canary Is*	140B4
Sergipe State *Brazil*	37F4	Sivas *Turk*	130B2	Stafford *Eng*	53E5
Sérifos *Greece*	81E3	Sjaelland I. *Den*	94C4	St. Albans *Eng*	56G6
Serov *Russia*	109H4	Skara *Sweden*	94C4	St. Andrews *Scot*	63F4
Serpukhov *Russia*	102E4	Skegness *Eng*	55H4	Stanley Falkland Is	39D8
Sérrai *Greece*	81E2	Skellefteå *Sweden*	93E3	Stara Zagora *Bulg*	83F2
Sétif *Alg*	141D4	Skíathos I. *Greece*	81E3	Starbuck I. *Kiribati*	162
Setúbal *Port*	73A2	Skien *Nor*	94B4	St. Austell *Eng*	59C7
Sevastopol' *Ukraine*	108E5	Skikda *Alg*	141D3	Stavanger *Nor*	94B4
Severnaya Zemlya		Skiros *Greece*	81E3	Stavropol' *Russia*	108F5
Russia	104L2	Skopélos *Greece*	81E3	St. Brieuc *France*	68B2
Severodvinsk *Russia*	102E3	Skopje *Mac*	82E2	St. Croix I.	
Sevilla *Spain*	73A2	Skovorodino *Russia*	106O4	*Caribbean Sea*	26F3
Seychelles Is. *Indian*	150F1	Skye I. *Scot*	60B3	St. David's *Wales*	58B6
Seydhisfrodhur *Iceland*	92C1	Slatina *Rom*	88E2	St. Denis *Réunion*	151F4
Sézanne *France*	70C2	Sligo *Ireland*	64C2	St. Dizier *France*	70C2
Sfax *Tunisia*	141E3	Sliven *Bulg*	83F2	Steinkjer *Nor*	92C3
'S-Gravenhage *Neth*	84A2	Sobral *Brazil*	37E3	St. Etienne *France*	71C2
Shado Shima I. *Japan*	115N7	Société, Is. de la		Stewart I. *NZ*	157F5
Shahjahanpur *India*	126G3	*French Pol*	165	St. Gaudens *France*	69C3
Shakhty *Russia*	108F5	Socotra I. *Rep Yemen*	133D4	St. George's *Grenada*	27G4
Shandong Province		Sodankylä *Fin*	93F2	St. Helens *Eng*	53E4
China	112F3	Södertälje *Sweden*	94D4	St. Helier *Jersey*	59E8
Shanghai *China*	114G3	Söderhamn *Sweden*	94D3	Stirling *Scot*	62E4
Shangrao *China*	114F4	Sofia *Bulg*	82E2	St. Ives *Eng*	59B7
Shantou *China*	114F4	Sokodé *Togo*	145D2	St. John *Canada*	15M5
Shanxi Province *China*	112F3	Sokoto *Nig*	145D1	St. John's *Antigua*	26G3
Shaoguan *China*	114F4	Solåpur *India*	128F4	St. John's *Canada*	15N5
Shaoxing *China*	114G4	Sollefteå *Sweden*	92D3	St. Kitts Is.	
Shaoyang *China*	114F4	Solomon Is. *Pacific O*	156F2	*Caribbean Sea*	26G3
Shapinsay I. *Scot*	61F1	Somerset I. *Canada*	14J2	St. Lawrence I. *USA*	22J
Shashi *China*	114F3	Sondrio *Italy*	76B1	St. Louis *Sen*	140B5
Sheffield *Eng*	55F4	Songkhla *Thai*	122C3	St. Louis *USA*	18D2
Shenyang *China*	112G2	Sorocaba *Brazil*	38F5	St. Lucia I.	
Shetland Is. *Scot*	61J7	Sorong *Indon*	124F4	*Caribbean Sea*	27G4
Shijiazhuang *China*	112F3	Soroti *Uganda*	146G4	St. Malo *France*	68B2
Shillong *India*	127H3	Sorrento *Italy*	79C2	St. Martin	
Shimizu *Japan*	115N9	Sorsele *Sweden*	92D2	*Caribbean Sea*	26G3
Shingū *Japan*	115L10	Sosnowiec *Pol*	88D2	St. Mary's *Eng*	59A8
Shiráz *Iran*	131D3	Souillac *France*	69C3	St. Nazaire *France*	68B2
Shizuoka *Japan*	115N9	Sŏul *S Korea*	112G3	St. Paul *USA*	18D1
Shkodër *Alb*	82D2	Sousse *Tunisia*	141E3	St. Peter Port *Guernsey*	59E8
Shreveport *USA*	20D2	Southampton I. *Canada*	14K3	St. Petersburg *Russia*	102E4
Shrewsbury *Eng*	58E5	Southampton *Eng*	56F7	St. Petersburg *USA*	20E3
Shuangyashan *China*	113H2	South Aust. State *Aus*	154C3	St. Quentin *France*	70C2
Sialkot *Pak*	126F2	South Carolina State		Stockport *Eng*	53E4
Siauliai *Lithuania*	95E5	*USA*	18E2	Stoke-on-Trent *Eng*	53E4
Sibenik *Cro*	77D2	South Dakota State		Stonehaven *Scot*	63F4
Siberut I. *Indon*	122B4	*USA*	17C1	Stören *Nor*	92C3
Sibiu *Rom*	88E3	Southend-on-Sea *Eng*	56H6	Storlien *Sweden*	92C3

Place	Ref	Place	Ref	Place	Ref
Stornoway Scot	60B2	Ta'izz Rep Yemen	132C4	Thíra I. Greece	81F3
Storuman Sweden	92D2	Takada Japan	115N8	Thival Greece	81E3
Strabane N Ire	65D2	Takaoka Japan	115M8	Thiviers France	69C2
Stralsund FRG	85C2	Takasaki Japan	115N8	Thon Buri Thai	118C2
Stranraer Scot	62D6	Takoradi Ghana	144B2	Thule Greenland	14M2
Strasbourg France	70D2	Talavera de la Reina		Thunder Bay Canada	15K5
Stratford-on-Avon Eng	56F5	Spain	72B2	Thurles Ireland	67D4
Streymoy I. Den	92A2	Talca Chile	40B6	Thurso Scot	61E2
Strömsund Sweden	92D3	Talcahuano Chile	40B6	Thurston I. Ant	170
Stronsay I. Scot	61F1	Tallahassee USA	20E2	Tianjin China	112F3
Stroud Eng	56E6	Tallinn Estonia	102D4	Tianshui China	117E3
St. Tropez France	71D3	Tamale Ghana	144B2	Tibet, Autonomous Region	
Stuttgart FRG	90B3	Tamanrasset Alg	141D4	China	116C3
St. Vincent I.		Tambacounda Sen	140B5	Tidjikkdja Maur	140B5
Caribbean Sea	27G4	Tampa USA	20E3	Tierp Sweden	94D3
Subotica Yugos	82D1	Tampere Fin	95E3	Tierra del Fuego I. Arg	41C8
Suceava Rom	89F3	Tampico Mexico	23D3	Tierra del Fuego State	
Sucre Bolivia	35C4	Tamworth Aust	157E4	Arg	41C8
Suduroy I. Den	92A2	Tanga Tanz	147G5	Tijuana USA	16B2
Suez Egypt	142G2	Tanger Mor	140C3	Tilburg Neth	84A2
Sukhumi Georgia	108F5	Tangshan China	112F3	Tilos Greece	81F3
Sukkur Pak	126E3	Tanna I. Vanuatu	156F2	Timbákion Greece	81E3
Sulawesi Indon	124E4	Tanta Egypt	142G1	Timimoun Alg	141D4
Sulu Arch. Phil	120E3	Taolanaro Madag	151E3	Timisoara Rom	88E3
Sumba I. Indon	123D4	Tarābulus Libya	141E3	Timor Indon	124E4
Sumbawa I. Indon	123D4	Tarakan Indon/Malay	123D3	Tindouf Alg	140C4
Sumen Bulg	83F2	Tarancón Spain	79B1	Tipperary Ireland	66C4
Sumy Ukraine	108E4	Taranto Italy	79D2	Tiranë Alb	80D2
Sunderland Eng	54F3	Tarbert Ireland	66B4	Tiree I. Scot	62B4
Sundsvall Sweden	92D3	Tarbert Scot	60B3	Tîrgu Mures Rom	89E3
Suntar Russia	106N3	Tarbert Scot	52B2	Tiruchiráppalli India	128F4
Surabaya Indon	123D4	Tarbes France	69C3	Titov Veles Macedonia	82E2
Surakarta Indon	123D4	Tarcoola Aust	155C4	Tlemcen Alg	141C3
Surat India	128F3	Tarfaya Mor	140B4	Toamasina Madag	150E2
Surgut Russia	109J3	Tarnów Pol	88E2	Tobago I.	
Surtsey I. Iceland	92A2	Tarragona Spain	74C1	Caribbean Sea	27G4
Suva Fiji	165	Tarrasa Spain	74C1	Tobermory Scot	62B4
Suzhou China	114G3	Tartung Indon	122B3	Tobol'sk Russia	109H4
Svalbard Is. Nor	103C2	Tashkent Uzbekistan	109H5	Tokelau Is. Pacific O	165
Sveg Sweden	94C3	Taunton Eng	58D6	Tokushima Japan	113H3
Sverdrup Is. Canada	12H2	Tavira Port	73A2	Tokyo Japan	115H9
Svetozarevo Yugos	82E2	Tavoy Myanmar	118B2	Toledo Spain	72B2
Swakopmund S Africa	149B3	Tawau Malay	123D3	Toledo USA	18E1
Swan I. Honduras	24C3	Tawitawi Phil	120E3	Toliara Madag	151E3
Swansea Wales	58D6	Tbilisi Georgia	108F5	Tombouctou Mali	140C5
Swaziland, Kingdom		Tecuci Rom	89F3	Tomsk Russia	109K4
Indep S Africa	151D3	Tegucigalpa Honduras	25B4	Tonbridge Eng	56H6
Swindon Eng	56F6	Tehrán Iran	131D2	Tonga Is. Pacific O	165
Sydney Aust	157E4	Tehuantepec Mexico	20D4	Tonghua China	112G2
Syktyvkar Russia	103G3	Tel Aviv Israel	130B2	Tongling China	114F3
Syracuse USA	18F1	Telford Eng	58E5	Tongue Scot	60D4
Syzran' Russia	108F4	Telukbetung Indon	123C4	Toowoomba Aust	156E3
Szczecin Pol	85C2	Temuco Chile	40B6	Topeka USA	17D2
Szczecinek Pol	85D2	Tenerife Canary Is	140B4	Tordesillas Spain	72A1
Szeged Hung	88E3	Tennant Creek Aust	154C2	Torino Italy	76B1
Székesfehérvár Hung	88D3	Tennessee State USA	18E2	Tornio Fin	93E2
Szekszárd Hung	88D3	Teófilo Otôni Brazil	37E4	Toronto Canada	15L5
Szolnok Hung	88E3	Teresina Brazil	37E3	Torquay Eng	59D7
		Termez Uzbekistan	109H6	Torreón Mexico	23C3
T		Termoli Italy	77C2	Torridon Scot	60C3
Tabora Tanz	146G5	Terni Italy	77C2	Tortosa Spain	74C1
Tabriz Iran	131C2	Teruel Spain	74B1	Tóshavn Faroes	92A2
Tabuaeran I. Kiribati	162	Tessalit Mali	141D4	Tottori Japan	115L9
Tabuk S Arabia	130B3	Tete Mozam	150D2	Touggourt Alg	141D3
Taegu S Korea	113G3	Tétouan Mor	140C3	Toulon France	71D3
Taejon S Korea	112G3	Teviothead Scot	63F5	Toulouse France	69C3
Tahiti I. Pacific O	162	Texas State USA	23C2	Tourcoing France	70C1
Tahoua Niger	145D1	Thásos I. Greece	81E2	Tours France	68C2
T'ai-pei Taiwan	120E1	Thetford Eng	56H5	Tovalu Is. Pacific O	165
Tái-nan Taiwan	120E1	Thiès Sen	140B5	Townsville Aust	156D2
Taiwan,Republic China	120E1	Thimphu Bhutan	127G3	Toyama Japan	115M8
Taiyuan China	112F3	Thionville France	70D2		

Place	Ref
Toyohashi *Japan*	115M9
Tozeur *Tunisia*	141D3
Trabzon *Turk*	130B1
Tralee *Ireland*	66B4
Trangan I. *Indon*	124F4
Trapani *Italy*	78C3
Trenton *USA*	19F1
Trincomalee *Sri Lanka*	129G5
Trinidad *Caribbean Sea*	27G4
Tripoli *Libya*	141E3
Tripolis *Greece*	80E3
Tromsö *Nor*	93D2
Trondheim *Nor*	92C3
Trowbridge *Eng*	59E6
Troyes *France*	70C2
Trujillo *Peru*	35B3
Truro *Eng*	59B7
Tsetserleg *Mongolia*	111E2
Tsuchiura *Japan*	115P8
Tsumeb *Namibia*	149B2
Tsuruga *Japan*	115M9
Tsuruoka *Japan*	115N7
Tuamotu Is. *Pacific*	162
Tubruq *Libya*	142F1
Tubuai Is. *Pacific O*	162
Tucson *USA*	23B2
Tucuman State *Arg*	40C5
Tudela *Spain*	74B1
Tula *Russia*	102E4
Tullamore *Ireland*	67D3
Tulsa *USA*	17D2
Tunis *Tunisia*	141E3
Turda *Rom*	88E3
Turks Is. *Caribbean Sea*	26E2
Turku *Fin*	95E3
Turneff Is. *Belize*	24B3
Tuticorin *India*	128F5
Tuvalu Is. *Pacific O*	165
Tuzla *Bos Herz*	82D2
Tver' *Russia*	102E4
Tyumen' *Russia*	109H4
Tyy *Spain*	72A1

U

Place	Ref
Uberaba *Brazil*	37E4
Udaipur *India*	128F3
Uddevalla *Sweden*	94C4
Ufa *Russia*	109G4
Uig *Scot*	60B3
Ujung Pandang *Indon*	123D4
Ukhta *Russia*	103G3
Ul'yanovsk *Russia*	108F4
Ulaanbaatar *Mongolia*	111E2
Ulan Ude *Russia*	106M4
Ullapool *Scot*	60C3
Ulm *FRG*	90B3
Umeå *Sweden*	93E3
Umtata *S Africa*	149C4
Ungava Pen. *Canada*	15L3
Unimark I. *USA*	22J
Unst I. *Scot*	61K7
Upington *S Africa*	149C3
Uppsala *Sweden*	94D4
Ural'sk *Kazakhstan*	108G4
Urgench *Uzbekistan*	108H5
Urosevac *Yugos*	82E2
Ürümqi *China*	110C2
Urziceni *Rom*	83F2
Üsküdar *Turk*	130A1
Ussuriysk *Russia*	107P5
Ust' Kamchatsk *Russia*	105S4
Ust' Nera *Russia*	105Q3

Place	Ref
Usti *Czech Rep*	91C2
Utah State *USA*	17B2
Utiel *Spain*	75B2
Utrecht *Neth*	84A2
Utsjoki *Fin*	93F2
Utsunomiya *Japan*	115N8

V

Place	Ref
Vaasa *Fin*	93E3
Vadodara *India*	128F3
Vaduz *Liech*	70D2
Valdepeñas *Spain*	73B2
Valence *France*	71C3
Valencia *Spain*	75B2
Valencia *Ven*	34C1
Valencia de Alcántara *Spain*	73A2
Valencia Region *Spain*	75B2
Valenciennes *France*	70C1
Valladolid *Spain*	72B1
Valledupar *Colombia*	34B1
Valletta *Malta*	141E3
Valls *Spain*	74C1
Valparaíso *Chile*	40B6
Vancouver *Canada*	13F5
Vancouver I. *Canada*	13F5
Vang *Nor*	94B3
Vännäs *Sweden*	93D3
Vannes *France*	68B2
Vantaa *Fin*	95F3
Vanuatu Is. *Pacific O*	156F2
Vârânasi *India*	127G3
Varazdin *Cro*	77D1
Vardö *Nor*	93G1
Varna *Bulg*	83F2
Varnamo *Sweden*	94C4
Västerås *Sweden*	94D4
Västervik *Sweden*	94D4
Vasto *Italy*	77C2
Växjö *Sweden*	94C4
Veliko Turnovo *Bul*	83F2
Vellore *India*	129F4
Veracruz *Mexico*	23D4
Vereeniging *S Africa*	149C3
Verin *Spain*	72A1
Vermont State *USA*	19F1
Versailles *France*	68C2
Vestmannaeyjar I. *Iceland*	92A2
Viana do Castelo *Port*	72A1
Vibo Valentia *Italy*	79D3
Victoria *China*	119D1
Victoria I. *Canada*	12G2
Victoria State *Aust*	157D4
Videle *Rom*	83F2
Vidin *Bulg*	82E2
Viella *Spain*	74C1
Vienna *Aust*	91D3
Vientiane *Laos*	118C2
Vierzon *France*	68C2
Vigo *Spain*	72A1
Vijayawada *India*	129G4
Vila *Vanuatu*	156F2
Vila Nova de Gaia *Por*	72A1
Vila Real *Port*	72A1
Villach *Aust*	91C3
Vilnius *Lithuania*	102D4
Viña del Mar *Chile*	40B6
Vinh *Viet*	119C2
Vinnitsa *Ukraine*	102D5
Virgin Is. *Caribbean Sea*	26G3
Virginia State *USA*	18F2

Place	Ref
Vis I. *Cro*	77D2
Visby *Sweden*	95D4
Vishakhapatnam *India*	129G4
Vitebsk *Belarus*	102E4
Viterbo *Italy*	77C2
Vitória *Brazil*	38F5
Vitoria *Spain*	72B1
Vitry-le-François *Fra*	70C2
Vladimir *Russia*	102F4
Vladivostok *Russia*	107P5
Vlorë *Alb*	80D2
Volgograd *Russia*	108F5
Vologda *Russia*	102F4
Vólos *Greece*	80E3
Vorkuta *Russia*	103H3
Voronezh *Russia*	108E4
Voroshilovgrad *Ukraine*	108E5
Voss *Nor*	94B3
Vranje *Yugos*	82E2
Vratsa *Bulg*	82E2
Vrbovsko *Cro*	77D1
Vrsac *Yugos*	82E1

W

Place	Ref
Wadi Halfa *Sudan*	142G2
Wad Medani *Sudan*	146G3
Wagga Wagga *Aust*	157D4
Wahiawa *Hawaiian Is*	22H
Waigeo I. *Indon*	124F4
Wailuka *Hawaiian Is*	22H
Wakayama *Japan*	115L9
Wake I. *Pacific O*	159
Wakkanai *Japan*	113J2
Wallis and Futuna Is. *Pacific O*	165
Walsall *Eng*	56F5
Walvis Bay *Namibia*	149B3
Wanganui *NZ*	157G4
Warangal *India*	128F4
Warley *Eng*	56F5
Warminster *Eng*	59E6
Warrnambool *Aust*	155D4
Warsaw *Pol*	86E2
Warwick *Eng*	56F5
Washington DC *USA*	19F2
Washington State *USA*	16A1
Waterford *Ireland*	67D4
Watford *Eng*	56G6
Wau *PNG*	125G4
Wau *Sudan*	146F4
Weifang *China*	112F3
Welkom *S Africa*	149C3
Wellesley Is. *Aust*	154C2
Wellington *NZ*	157G5
Welshpool *Wales*	58D5
Wenzhou *China*	114G4
Wesel *FRG*	84B2
Wessel Is. *Aust*	154C2
West Bromwich *Eng*	56F5
West Falkland I. *South Atlantic*	41C8
West Indies,Is. *Caribbean Sea*	26F2
Weston-super-Mare *Eng*	58E6
Westport *Ireland*	64B3
Westray I. *Scot*	61E1
West Virginia State *USA*	18E2
Wetar I. *Indon*	124E4
Wewak *PNG*	125G4

Wexford *Ireland*	67E4
Weymouth *Eng*	59E7
Whalsay I. *Scot*	61K7
Whangarei *NZ*	157G4
Whitby *Eng*	55G3
Whitchurch *Eng*	53E5
Whitehaven *Eng*	53D3
Whitehorse *Canada*	12E3
Whyalla *Aust*	155C4
Wichita *USA*	17D2
Wick *Scot*	61E2
Wicklow *Ireland*	67E4
Widnes *Eng*	53E4
Wigan *Eng*	53E4
Wilhelmshaven *FRG*	84B2
Wilmington *USA*	19F2
Wilmslow *Eng*	53E4
Winchester *Eng*	56F6
Windhoek *Namibia*	149B3
Windsor *Eng*	56G6
Winnemucca *USA*	16A1
Winnipeg *Canada*	13J5
Wisconsin State *USA*	18D1
Wloclawek *Pol*	86D2
Wokam I. *Indon*	124F4
Wolfsburg *FRG*	85C2
Wollongong *Aust*	157E4
Wolverhampton *Eng*	58E5
Wŏnsan *N Korea*	112G3
Worcester *Eng*	58E5
Worcester *S Africa*	149B4
Workington *Eng*	52D3
Worksop *Eng*	55F4
Worthing *Eng*	57G7
Wrexham *Wales*	53E4
Wroclaw *Pol*	91D2
Wuhan *China*	114F3
Wuhu *China*	114F3
Würzburg *FRG*	90B3
Wuxi *China*	114G3
Wuzhou *China*	114F4
Wyndham *Aust*	154B2
Wyoming State *USA*	17C1

X

Xai Xai *Mozam*	151D3
Xi'an *China*	117E3

Xiamen *China*	114F4
Xiangfan *China*	114F3
Xiangtan *China*	114F4
Xingtai *China*	112F3
Xining *China*	111E3
Xinjiang Uygur Zizhiqu Prov. *China*	110C2
Xinxiang *China*	114F3
Xinyang *China*	114F3
Xuchang *China*	114F3
Xuzhou *China*	114F3

Y

Ya'an *China*	117E3
Yakutsk *Russia*	104O3
Yamagata *Japan*	115P7
Yamdena I. *Indon*	124F4
Yamoussoukro *Côte d'Ivoire*	144B2
Yangon *Myanmar*	118B2
Yangquan *China*	112F3
Yangzhou *China*	114F3
Yantai *China*	112G3
Yaoundé *Cameroon*	145E4
Yap I. *Pacific O*	121F3
Yapen I. *Indon*	125F4
Yaroslavl' *Russia*	102E4
Yazd *Iran*	131D2
Ye *Myanmar*	118B2
Yekaterinburg *Russia*	109H4
Yell I. *Scot*	61J7
Yellowknife *Canada*	12G3
Yeniseysk *Russia*	106L4
Yeovil *Eng*	58E7
Yerevan *Armenia*	108F5
Yibin *China*	117E4
Yichang *China*	114F3
Yinchuan *China*	111E3
Yingkou *China*	112G2
Yiyang *China*	114F4
Yogyakarta *Indon*	123D4
Yokkaichu *Japan*	115M9
Yokohama *Japan*	115N9
Yokosuka *Japan*	115N9
York *Eng*	55F4
Youghal *Ireland*	67D4

Ystad *Sweden*	94C4
Yukon Territory State *Canada*	12E3
Yumen *China*	111D2
Yunnan Province *China*	117E4
Yuzhno-Sakhalinsk *Russia*	107Q5

Z

Zaandam *Neth*	84A2
Zadar *Cro*	77D2
Zafra *Spain*	73A2
Zagreb *Cro*	77D1
Záhedān *Iran*	131E3
Zákinthos I. *Greece*	80E3
Zamboanga *Phil*	120E3
Zamora *Spain*	72A1
Zanzibar I. *Tanz*	147G5
Zaporozh'ye *Ukraine*	108E5
Zaragón Region *Spain*	74B1
Zaragoza *Spain*	74B1
Zaysan *Kazakhstan*	109K5
Zemlya Frantsa Iosifa Is. *Barents Sea*	103G1
Zenica *Bos Herz*	82D2
Zhangjiakou *China*	112F2
Zhangzhou *China*	114F4
Zhanjiang *China*	114F4
Zhejiang Province *China*	114F4
Zhengzhou *China*	114F3
Zhenjiang *China*	114F3
Zhitomir *Ukraine*	102D4
Zhuzhou *China*	114F4
Zibo *China*	112F3
Zielona Gora *Pol*	85D2
Ziguinchor *Sen*	140B5
Zilina *Slovakia*	88D3
Zinder *Niger*	145D1
Zlatoust *Russia*	109G4
Znojmo *Czech Rep*	91D3
Zomba *Malawi*	150D2
Zouerate *Maur*	140B4
Zunyi *China*	117E4
Zurich *Switz*	70D2
Zwickau *FRG*	91C2

Published by Geddes & Grosset, an imprint of
Children's Leisure Products Limited

© 1998 Children's Leisure Products Limited,
David Dale House, New Lanark ML11 9DJ, Scotland

First published 1998
Reprinted 1999

ISBN 1 85534 326 6

Printed and bound in the UK